An Introduction to
the Writings of Ngugi

G. D. Killam

Professor of English
University of Guelph

LONDON
HEINEMANN
IBADAN NAIROBI

Heinemann Educational Books Ltd
22 Bedford Square, London WC1B 3HH
P.M.B. 5205, Ibadan P.O. Box 45314, Nairobi

EDINBURGH MELBOURNE AUCKLAND
HONG KONG SINGAPORE KUALA LUMPUR NEW DELHI
KINGSTON PORT OF SPAIN

Heinemann Educational Books Inc.
4 Front Street, Exeter, New Hampshire 03833, USA

For Sach and Sarah

British Library Cataloguing in Publication Data

Killam, Gordon Douglas
    An introduction to the writings of Ngugi – (Studies in
    African Literature).
    1. Ngugi wa Thiong'o – Criticism and interpretation.
    I. Title   II. Series
    823   PR9381 .9 .N45Z/

    ISBN 0-435-91669-6

Set, printed and bound in Great Britain by
Whitstable Litho Ltd, Whitstable, Kent

Contents

▼▼▼▼▼▼▼▼▼▼▼▼▼▼▼▼▼▼▼▼▼▼▼▼▼▼▼▼

Foreword

▼▼▼▼▼▼▼▼▼▼▼▼▼▼▼▼▼▼▼▼▼▼▼▼▼▼▼▼▼▼▼▼▼▼▼▼▼▼

This book is a critical introduction to Ngugi's writing to date. It is neither complete nor definitive. Ngugi is still alive, and after a period of imprisonment, well. So it is likely that a man at the height of his creative powers will continue to write. He has given some indication that his medium may no longer be 'Afro-Saxon', as he calls the English language used by African practitioners. But whether or not that is the case, any attempt at a definitive account of his achievement as a writer to date would be premature. Nevertheless, there is a pause in his writing occasioned partly by his imprisonment and partly by his opinions about which language he should use to serve the literary and social purposes he conceives his role to be. We can fill that pause with this study.

The opinions offered here on the works are my own, except for the introductory chapter, but even so I have profited a good deal from reading such criticism of Ngugi's work as exists and have made a note where indebtedness is direct. The exception is the first chapter which deals with Ngugi's life and with the growth of his literary reputation as this is defined by critics over the course of the last fifteen or so years.

It seems plain that a writer with an intensity of purpose and command of his craft such as Ngugi possesses will continue to write. It remains to be seen whether that writing will be done in English or in an African language, possibly Swahili, possibly Gikuyu.

Ngugi wa Thiong'o

Biographical Outline

▼▼▼▼▼▼▼▼▼▼▼▼▼▼▼▼▼▼▼▼▼▼▼▼▼▼▼▼▼▼

1938	(James) Ngugi wa Thiong'o born at Kamarithu, Limuru, Kenya on 5 January.
1947	Primary school education begins at Gukuyu Kariug'a School, Kamundura, Limuru.
1954	Enters Alliance High School, Kikuyu.
1959	Enters Makerere University College, Kampala, Uganda. Remained there until 1964.
1962	*The Black Hermit* performed as part of Uganda's independence celebration.
1963-4	Editor *Penpoint*.
1964	*Weep Not, Child* published.
1964	Joins staff of *The Sunday Nation* in Nairobi.
1964	Enters Leeds University, UK.
1965	*The River Between* published.
1966	First prize, 'Negro Arts Festival of Dakar', for *Weep Not, Child.*
1967	*A Grain of Wheat* published.
1968	Appointed lecturer, Department of English, University College, Nairobi.
1969	Resigns lecturership in protest against government interference with Academic Freedom in the University.
1969	Enters Northwestern University, USA.
1970	'This Time Tomorrow', E.A.L.B., reprinted in *Short African Plays*, ed. Cosmo Pieterse (London: Heinemann Educational Books, 1972).
1971	Returns to Nairobi as lecturer in the Literature Department, University of Nairobi.
1972	*Homecoming* published.
1972	Becomes Acting Head of the Department of Literature, University of Nairobi.
1976	*The Trial of Dedan Kimathi* (with Micere Githae Mugo) published.

1977	*Petals of Blood* published.
1977	*Ngaahika Ndeenda* performed.
1977	Placed in detention by Kenyan Police on 31 December.
1978	Released from detention on 12 December.
1980	*Ngaahika Ndeenda* published.
1980	*Caitaani Mutharaba-Ini* published.

1 Introduction

▼▼▼▼▼▼▼▼▼▼▼▼▼▼▼▼▼▼▼▼▼▼▼▼▼▼▼▼▼▼▼

K ENYA'S best-known writer was born at Limuru, near Nairobi,
in 1938. He was called James Ngugi until March 1970, when he
took the new and traditional Kikuyu name, Ngugi wa Thiong'o.
This is worth stating for anybody who still does not know that novels,
plays, short stories and articles published under the name of James Ngugi
are from the hand of Ngugi wa Thiong'o. Ime Ikiddeh, who has written
the introduction to Ngugi's *Homecoming* essays, explains the circumstances of the conversion thus:

> 'I am not a man of the Church. I am not even a Christian.' Those were the
> stunning words with which James Ngugi opened his talk to the Fifth General
> Assembly of the Presbyterian Church of East Africa in Nairobi in March, 1970.
> The talk reproduced in this collection as 'Church, Culture and Politics'. He had
> hardly ended his address when a wiry old man, visibly choking with anger, leapt
> to the floor, and, shaking his walking-stick menacingly toward the front,
> warned the speaker to seek immediate repentance in prayer. The old man did
> not forget to add as a reminder that in spite of his shameless denial and all his
> blasphemy, the speaker *was* a Christian and the evidence was his first name.
> Ngugi had never given serious thought to his contradiction. Now it struck him
> that perhaps the old man had a point, and the name James, an unfortunate
> anomaly, had to go'.[1]

In any case, Ngugi's reputation as a|writer is so well established now, that
he is referred to as Ngugi and it little matters whether that is a 'Christian'
or a surname. Ngugi had his early education in a primary school near his
village and then at a Gikuyu independent school, also nearby. (Gikuyu
independent schools were founded and operated by Kikuyu people who
had rebelled against missionary influence; their aim was to provide
education of a kind appropriate to the African setting.) Subsequent to this
he went to a missionary school. He documents this quite fully and it is
worth hearing him on the subject for the light his words throw on his later
work as an imaginative writer. In an interview with Alan Marcuson at
Leeds in England, Ngugi says of the missionary schools and missionary
teachers:

> As I see them in their ... historical role, they have been the forerunners of

colonialism . . . the John the Baptists preparing the way for Christ – the colonial administration . . . I found white people, missionaries, were very kind, very peaceful, and they wanted to help you, but in a very patronising manner. The Headmaster was said to be pro-African, but he believed, and often told us so, that there was not a single African in the whole of Kenya, who on the basis of merit could qualify to Cambridge. As an African you could be taken in Cambridge but not on basis of merit, more as a gesture. Of course, we protested, but inwardly we believed it, and unconsciously had a high regard for the white boys.[2]

After secondary school, Ngugi went to Kampala, to Makerere College. At that time still a university college of London, Makerere College was the oldest of the university colleges of East Africa and the only one at the time Ngugi went there that offered a degree in English Literature. Ngugi sees university education in East Africa at that time as an extension of the colonial education introduced in the missionary schools. He says:

You must see universities in Africa in their colonialist missionary setting. They didn't want you to question things, or compare western institutions with other systems. For instance, those who studied Political Science heard of Karl Marx only as an incidental rather eccentric figure. You would never have thought he was one of the people whose doctrine has influenced two-thirds of the world. African History was taught merely as an extension of Europe. One or two of the lecturers were enlightened, but they nearly all believed that the only real education was to be found in Britain. Literature has nothing or very little to do with what was happening in Africa. So, in novels and plays we learned about British people. And even then we learned about them not in terms of social issues, but in terms of universal values and the tragedy of a human being caught in a situation whose conditions he cannot control.[3]

One sees in this appreciation of the forms and functions of colonial education policy in Africa, the circumstances which induced Ngugi with his colleagues at Nairobi in 1968 to advocate the total revision of the syllabus in the Literature Department, something we will have occasion to mention again shortly. One presumes, as well, that these experiences at Makerere and the thoughts Ngugi has had on them since that time shaped his policy as Head of the Department of Literature at the University of Nairobi.

Ngugi read English in the honours programme at Makerere and it was there that he first began to write in an imaginative way, something which he had wanted to do while in secondary school, but had not got around to doing. He describes his first efforts at imaginative writing in the preface to *Secret Lives*:

Sometime in 1960 I met Mr Jonathan Kariara outside the Main Hall of Makerere University College and on an impulse stopped him: I had written a short story and would he care to look at it? Mr Kariara was then in his final year as a student of English: he was very involved in *Penpoint*, a journal then at the centre of the creative efforts on Makerere Hill. I had told him a lie. I was then in my secondary preliminary year, and the story was only in my mind. But with my impulsive lie, I knew I had to write a story.[4]

His first complete piece of writing was 'The Fig Tree' which appears as 'Mugumo' in the short story collection. This was the period, as well, of the writing and production of *The Black Hermit* which was produced by the Uganda National Theatre in November 1962. The notices of the play brought public attention to Ngugi for the first time and we will have occasion to look at these critical responses. The play was not published until 1968 when Ngugi had an established reputation as a novelist, and it has never provoked the same interest his novels have. Nevertheless, he continues to write plays and it is an irony that while his first play was judged unsuccessful, his latest one was so successful – in one manner of speaking – that it provoked the authorities in Kenya to arrest him.

Ngugi was a student at Makerere College when one of the earliest gatherings of African writers was held there in 1962. He makes no mention of his reactions to this meeting anywhere, but in light of the delegates who attended, most of whom had already made their marks as writers, it was likely that he had aspirations for a writing career confirmed. Among those who attended and read papers were Chinua Achebe, Wole Soyinka, Christopher Okigbo and J.P. Clark. Discussion ranged over a wide variety of topics. Among them was the attempt to formulate a definition of African Literature. Proceedings were reported in the press and in various journals devoted to African affairs. What must have caught Ngugi's notice in light of his subsequent writing and especially in light of his assertions about the role of the writer, were papers devoted to the subject of the social purposes of contemporary writing from Africa.

Ngugi graduated from Makerere College in 1964. He worked for a time on Nairobi's *Daily Nation* and then left East Africa to pursue graduate work at the University of Leeds. When he returned to Africa Ngugi was appointed Special Lecturer in the Department of English at the University College in Nairobi, a position he held for a year and a half. There was a student strike in January of 1969 and he resigned his post as a protest against the college's closure on 27 January, discerning along with many of his colleagues, a dictatorial attitude on the part of the university administration toward the student body both during and after the strike. It was at this time, as well, that he, along with Taban Lo Liyong and Henry Owuor-Anyumba, formulated the proposal on the 'Abolition of the English Department'. This attracted considerable attention. The force of the proposal and its radical nature in the context of the climate of the university at the time, is specified in its concluding paragraphs. The three authors sum up their recommendation in this fashion:

> One of the things which has been hindering a radical outlook in our study of literature in Africa is the question of literary excellence that only works of undisputed literary excellence should be offered (in this case it meant virtually the study of disputable 'peaks' of English Literature). The question of literary excellence implies a value judgement of what is literary and what is excellence, and from whose point of view. For any group it is better to study representative works which mirror their society rather than to study a few isolated 'classics', either of their own or of a foreign culture.
>
> We have been trying all along to place values where they belong. We have argued the case for the abolition of the present Department of English in the College, and the establishment of the Department of African Literature and Languages. This is not a change of names only. We want to establish the centrality of Africa in the Department. This, we have argued, is justifiable on various grounds, the most important one being that education is a means of knowledge about ourselves ... The dominant object in that perspective is African Literature, the major branch of African culture. Its roots go back to past African Literature, European Literature, and Asian Literature. These can only be studied meaningfully in a Department of African Literature and Languages in an African university.[5]

After the controversy which provoked his resignation, Ngugi went overseas again, this time to Northwestern University, USA, where he taught and studied, and worked at writing his fourth novel, *Petals of Blood*. It is interesting to note in passing that virtually all of his imaginative writing, and certainly the major works, have been written outside Kenya. Ngugi himself has noted this. He returned to Kenya in 1970 and took up a second appointment in the Literature Department in the University of Nairobi. He assumed the headship in 1972.

Petals of Blood was published in June 1977, and launched in Nairobi with simultaneous publication in London. It is understandable, given its themes and treatments, that it provoked strong reaction. Doubtless that was what the author hoped for. Newspaper reviews in Nairobi hailed the novel with such comments as 'a literary bombshell', 'the most hard-hitting novel criticizing contemporary Kenyan society written since Independence'. A number of reviews noted that the novel would likely displease many of those who had been victims of Ngugi's pen in the past. But Ngugi apparently foresaw no difficulty, saying that criticism of the kind he was offering was healthy in a society since it might provoke debate which would bring about necessary change.

The book was widely reviewed overseas and most of the reviews were enthusiastic. All of them recognized the force of Ngugi's condemnation of the current political regime in the novel and felt the force of his indignation over the betrayal of the independence movement.

Ngaahika Ndeenda, translated into English, means 'I will marry when I choose' – the play that was banned and was responsible for landing Ngugi in jail, is not in an English version. As reported in various newspapers the story it tells us is as follows. Kigunda is a poor labourer who works on Kioi's farm. Kioi is a strong Christian and member of the Muhonoki, a revivalist movement. He is also very rich. He has a partner named Ikuaa. Kioi and Ikuaa want to take Kigunda's little bit of land away from him because they have plans to build a factory in partnership with foreign investors to make insecticide. Kioi and his wife persuade Kigunda to obtain a bank loan against the security of his land so that he can have his marriage 'cleansed' in a Christian church. While this is happening a sub-plot describes the relationship of Kigunda's daughter and Kioi's son, John Muhuni. When he makes her pregnant Muhuni deserts the girl. Kigunda is duped as Kioi hoped he would be. Unable to pay back the money he has used to 'renew' his marriage to Wangechi, he loses the land to Kioi who buys it at an auction. At the close of the play Kigunda is comforted by his friend Gichamba who works in a foreign-owned factory. It is difficult and improper to comment on the play without a copy of the text. But if the summary of the themes and treatments of the play is corrected – it is derived from a report in the Nairobi *Weekly Review* – then it is safe to say in the play Ngugi and his collaborator are concerned with the same themes that inform *Petals of Blood, The Trial of Dedan Kimathi* and the stories in the final section of *Secret Lives*.

Anyone who had followed the development of his career, both as author and as a person concerned with public life, should not have been surprised at the substance of the new novel. Ngugi has felt from the outset of his career as a writer that writing should serve social and political purposes. Themes are apparent in the first play, which, for all of its weaknesses, dramatize the question of responsibility in a contemporary setting. Some of the naivety of the play's political thought can be accounted for by the youthfulness of its author; part because there was reason to have genuine optimism over the potential inherent in Uhuru celebrations. His purposes for writing are plain in the novels: each examines the consequences of public, political events as they affect the lives of individual members of the community.

Ngugi's convictions about the functions of the writer have been remarkably consistent in their development. He tells us in an interview with fellow students at Leeds[6] that he very early on saw the confining effect of a Eurocentric education, that this effect was recognized by his parents who contributed to the development of a Kikuyu school which the young Ngugi attended. More than this he saw the effect of the subservient position of his father to an African landlord: such circumstances as these helped to bring about the Mau Mau crisis in the early 1950s, a situation which is dramatized in *Weep Not, Child* through the events which shape and destroy the life of Ngotho and his family. Ngugi has stated his belief about the position of the writer in a variety of places but nowhere is it better summed up than in the essays in *Homecoming* (published in 1972) in the author's note which, he says, were written concurrently with the production of the first three novels. He articulates his belief about literature and its place in society. In defining his own role as writer he notes that in the essay the writer can be more direct, didactic and polemical than he can be in the creative process where he is in the world of imagination. These statements extrapolated from the text of the author's note when put together in a series such as follows, provide the *apologia pro sua vita* of Ngugi, the writer. He says: 'Literature does not grow or does not develop in a vacuum; it is given impetus, shape, direction and even area of concern by social, political and economic forces in a particular society . . . There is no area of our lives which has not been affected by the social, political and expansionist needs of European capitalism . . .'[7] In becoming more specific about the function of literature, Ngugi writes:

> Literature is, of course, primarily concerned with what any political and economic arrangement does to the spirit and values governing human relationship. Nobody who has passed through the major cities of Europe and America, where Capitalism is in full bloom, can ever wish the same fate on Africa as far as human relationships are concerned . . . It is the height of irony that we, who have suffered most from exploitation, are now supporting a system that not only continues that basic exploitation, but exacerbates destructive rivalries between brothers and sisters, a system that thrives on the survival instincts of dwellers in a Darwinian jungle. The writer cannot be exempted from the task of exposing the distorted values governing such a jungle precisely because this distorts healthy human relationships.[8]

The novels therefore become a creative manifestation of this exploration of beliefs. Ngugi says in another place that the novels, the stories and the plays 'form my creative autobiography over the last twelve years and touch on ideas and moods affecting me over the same period. My writing is really an attempt to understand myself and my situation in society and in history'.[9]

Yet for all his assertion over the specific social role that his fiction and the plays are meant to have, the artist controls the didactic or polemical elements in the fiction. Here we can trust the teller *and* the tale. The essays and the creative writing are companion pieces, the one explicating the other. Ngugi is consistent in the attention he pays to his basic themes; the more he thinks on the implications of those aspects of the Kenyan experience of the forces of imperialism and colonialism – the more his vision sharpens – the more his invention goes to work on the imaginative presentation. In the author's note he identifies three phases of the encounter with European imperialism – 'slavery', 'colonialism' and 'neo-colonialism'. The first two novels deal with the period of slavery and colonialism, the enslavement taking various forms from the physical control a superior power is able to manifest over a people, to the more subtle control perpetrated and perpetuated through ideas. The essay on 'Church, Culture and Politics' is apposite here. Obviously there is a good deal of overlapping in the novels in the way in which the three phases Ngugi identifies are treated.

But Ngugi's position has altered very little from the outset of his writing career as can be seen in an interview which he gave in the *Black Books Bulletin* in August of 1978, printed obviously after he had been arrested by agents of the Kenyan government. He said:

> Because racism does not emanate from some biological arrangement, I must assume that it can be changed. We can see racism as a phenomenon that has social, political, and economic bases and origins and is thus, subject to social, political and economic solutions. Black people have been victims of double exploitation. They have been exploited on the level of class because they constitute the majority of the working class and the laboring masses. They have also been exploited on the dimension of race because of the whole colonial context in which Black and White people have met. Thus, Black people must realize themselves on the level of class and take anti-capitalist and anti-imperialist positions. Also, they must proclaim their color with pride, their culture with pride, their history with pride, their whole past with pride![10]

I want to consider briefly four aspects of Ngugi's non-fictional writing which have a direct bearing on his fiction. These are his statements on the Christian Church and its specific influence and its relationship to colonial government and education, on how history works in his society under the stress of forces from the outside, on the question of the adoption of a foreign language, and finally, on the literary and political thinkers who have influenced him in his writing.

His first novel, *The River Between*, was written, he tells us, when he was a devout Christian and when he was still a student at Makerere College. The importance of Christian teaching is apparent in all of his writing. Recognizing it as a force and influence in his society, he is bound to take it into account in his writing. There will be occasion to consider how the life in his novels is shaped by the presence of Christianity. But it is worth noting at this point what Ngugi thinks of the effect of Christianity in the abstract.

There are a series of related reasons why Ngugi abandoned the Christian faith and these are expressed succinctly in the essay 'Church, Culture and Politics'. In historical terms he says that while he cannot escape the influence of the church because it is all around him he is, nevertheless, aware of the contradiction inherent in 'colonialism and its religious ally, the Christian Church'. He goes on: 'I say contradiction because Christianity, whose basic doctrine was love and equality between men, was an integral part of that social force – colonialism – which in Kenya was built on the inequality and hatred between men and the consequent subjugation of the black race by the white race'.[11] The consequence of the teaching of the Christian missionaries meant that African customs were rejected outright. He continues:

> It meant rejection of these values and rituals that held us together: it meant adopting what, in effect, was a debased European middle-class mode of living and behaviour. The European missionary had attacked the primitive rights of our people, had condemned our beautiful African dances, the images of our Gods, recoiling from their suggestion of satanic sensuality. The African convert did the same, often with even greater zeal, for he had to prove how Christian he was through this rejection of his past and roots.[12]

Ngugi notes how, traditionally, the Christian Church has aligned itself with the ruling class and given the lie to its own protestations of support for a humanistic vision of life. The church, claims Ngugi, has always been in alliance with the ruling class and adjusted its precepts to suit the needs of that class, thus guaranteeing its own safety and security. The essay, then, becomes a plea for the church in Africa to adjust itself to local conditions and an admonishment against letting happen to it what happened in Europe over the course of the centuries. With reference to the need to adjust to local conditions, Ngugi writes:

> If the Church in the past has been the greatest cause of the mis-shaping of African souls in cultural alienation, it must, today, work for cultural integration. It must go back to the roots of the broken African civilisation. It must examine the traditional African forms of marriage, traditional African forms of sacrifice. Why were these things meaningful and wholesome to the traditional African community?[13]

In the roots of the indigenous culture the real meaning for African peoples lies. Ngugi writes:

But, ultimately the African Church's greatest danger is in its area of social involvement. After Independence, African middle-class was born: this class is busy, grabbing and amassing land and business concerns at the expense of the peasant and working masses ... Will the Church, as happened in Europe and Latin America, form an alliance with this bureaucratic, commercial middle-class élite, the members of which, in any case, act as agents of foreign capitalism? Can the Church as a body reject the exploitation of the masses by a few who, because of the benefits of education and control of social institutions, are in a position to amass so much wealth? Will the Church reject capitalism, which is being found wasteful and inhuman?[14]

In the fictional evocations in the novels of Christian influence one notes that the disposition to view charitably the inefficacy of Christian teaching which brings about the destruction of Waiyaki and the disaffection of Njoroge, is replaced by the bitter repudiation of the faith as found in the denunciation Munira hurls at his father and the Rev. Jerrod at the close of *Petals of Blood*. Christianity, for Ngugi, is, then:

part and parcel of cultural imperialism. Christianity, in the past, has been used to rationalize imperialist domination and exploitation of peasants and workers. It has been used to blind people to the reality of their exploitation because Christianity as a whole wants to tell people that their lot is God-given, as opposed to man-conditioned. So, you see, if you are poor because God has willed it, you are more than likely to continue to pray to God to right your condition. But if you know that your poverty is not God-conditioned, but is socially conditioned, then you are likely to do something about those social conditions that are assuring that you be poor.[15]

It is this process of discovery about the consequences of adopting the Christian faith that caused Ngugi, by degrees, to abandon it, the abandonment culminating in the speech he gave to the Presbyterian Senate in Nairobi in 1970.

The church in Kenya, as it was over all of Africa during the imperial period, was in the vanguard in bringing about irreversible historical change. Ngugi traces this influence against the backdrop of some seventy-five years of Kenyan history in his novels.

In *A Celebration of Black and African Writing*, in a chapter entitled 'Ngugi wa Thiong'o: the novelist as historian',[16] Ime Ikiddeh elaborates fully the historical background against which Ngugi's novels are written and documents a good deal of the detail that finds its way into Ngugi's work. Ikiddeh takes a position midway between two predominating reactions to the historical content in Ngugi's work. One view is given expression by W. H. Jordan who regards 'the historical element in the novels as unartistic and objectionable interventions';[17] the other is represented by such a critic as S. N. Ngubiah who 'complains that the writer is not always faithful to widely accepted historical "fact".[18] We are

dealing in this book with the product of the creative evocation of a society over a sixty-year span and presented in four novels which can form a sequence for the very reason that they do draw on documented historical fact as background. Nevertheless we are dealing with works of the imagination which are not bound to be completely faithful to accepted historical fact. What Ngugi wants to do, as he makes plain in *Homecoming*, is evoke an awareness of the human reactions to the social and political circumstances which dictate the direction and quality of the lives of men and thus shape their history. Ikiddeh's assessment is important because in it he draws the attention of readers to the documented historical facts which are important to Ngugi's writing, thus clearing the way for readers to look at the novels as works of literature and not as works of simulated history. Ngugi's own view of the place of history in his work can be summed up quite well in this quotation from an interview which appeared shortly after the publication of *Petals of Blood* and dated 9 January 1978. Ngugi says in response to one of the questions in the interview:

> History is very important in any people, how we look at our past is very important in determining how we look at and how we evaluate the present. A distorted view of the people's past can very easily distort our views and evaluations of the present as well as the evaluation of our present potentials and the future possibilities as a people. Our history up to now has been distorted by the cultural needs of Imperialism, that is, it was in the interest of the Imperialists to distort Kenya history with the view of showing that Kenya people have not struggled with nature and with other men to change their natural environment and create a positive social environment. It was also in the interest of the Imperialists to show that the Kenya people had not resisted foreign domination. It was also in the interest of Imperialism to implement missionaries and other agents of Imperialism in bright colours and they did all these things using the terms of seeming objectivity. Now, I feel that Kenya writers, intellectuals, historians, political scientists must be able to show us Kenya's past which correctly evaluates Kenya's people achievement in the past, in the present and at the same time, pointing out their creative potential in the future.[19]

There are many similarities between Ngugi and his Nigerian contemporary Achebe who treats the theme of history in his novels. Achebe believes that the theme of history must be disposed of before he can proceed to look at the present. Ngugi, recognizing the need to look at the past for reasons stated in the quotation cited above, nevertheless uses history in a way different from Achebe. There will be occasion to look at his treatment of history as we consider each of the novels in light of their perception of history, but it is important to note now the fundamental difference in treatment. Obviously it is this special condition of Kenya in the colonial period which accounts for the greater urgency, the accelerated pace that one finds in Ngugi's novels. There is nothing of the leisureliness of Achebe novels in Ngugi's writing. Nothing of the sense of the inevitableness of the process of history; little of the disinterestedness of Achebe's treatment. His concern, moreover, is focused on the present almost with the fear that he will not be able to treat this 'present' before a new and more urgent 'present' has arisen.

Ngugi is concerned with the history of his people and seeks to extrapolate from his consideration of the influence of Europe on Kenya the means for making a better future. There are two predominating influences on his third and fourth novels. These are Karl Marx and, especially, Frantz Fanon. It is Marx who articulates a political and economic philosophy which will suit Ngugi's conviction about post-independent Kenyan development. It is Fanon who places the thinking of Marx in the African context. A number of critics of Ngugi's work have noted the shaping influence of Frantz Fanon on Ngugi's fiction. Ngugi cites Fanon in the important article 'Satire in Nigeria' which was published in the *Protest and Conflict* volume, where he writes, saying that Soyinka 'is dissatisfied with the new men in power, he has no patience with what Frantz Fanon, in his book, *The Wretched of the Earth*, has described as the shocking anti-national ways of a "bourgeoisie which is stupidly, contemptibly, cynically bourgeois". He is particularly incensed with the hypocrisy of religious leaders and with the ineffectuality and sheer apathy of the intellectuals'.[20] And Peter Nazareth says in an article '*A Grain of Wheat*: a socialist novel?' that Ngugi was introduced to Fanon's work by Grant Kamenju at the time when Ngugi was 'lying quiescent just before crossing what Conrad calls "The Shadow Line" between his early work and what was to become his mature work',[21] just at the point when he was to begin work on *A Grain of Wheat*. Kamenju, a fellow Kenyan and sometime Professor of Literature in the University of Dar es Salaam, has written on Fanon in an important article, 'Black aesthetics and pan-African emancipation'. Kamenju extrapolates a number of Fanon's premises for the purposes of testing Okot p'Bitek's achievement in *The Song of Lawino*. The general statements which Kamenju makes about Fanon have a bearing on Ngugi's novels and it is useful to list them here. Kamenju cites Fanon as saying that 'Black people as a people ... (national independence notwithstanding) continued to remain in chains culturally as well as economically and politically'; and hence as a people 'in whose heart an inferiority complex has been created by the death and burial of its local cultural originality'.[22] Fanon traces 'the black man's cultural and hence his aesthetic subjugation to its roots in imperialism and, especially to colonialism's most insidious weapon which is the cultural genocide of the colonised'. Kamenju notes in this record that 'Imperialism deploys into its active support and service the intellectual and cultural arsenals at its disposal. It is here that the cultural agent of imperialism in the person of the intellectual obscuranist, the racist anthropologist and the Christian missionary, apostles of civility and submission find their roles and come into their own'.[23] This is what Fanon calls the Manichean nature of the colonial world. Kamenju quotes Fanon at length from *The Wretched of the Earth*:

> It is not enough for the colonised to delimit physically, that is to say with the help of the army and the police force, the place of the native. As if Tutscho, the totalitarian character of colonial exploitation, the coloniser paints the native as a sort of quintessence of evil. Native society is not simply described as a society lacking in values. It is not enough for the colonist to affirm that those values have disappeared from, or still better, never existed in, the colonial world. A native is declared insensible to ethics; he represents not only the absence of values, but also the negation of values. He is, let us dare to admit it, the enemy of values and in this sense he is the absolute evil. He is the corrosive element destroying all that comes near him; he is the deforming element, disfiguring all that has to do with beauty or morality ... All values, in fact, are irrevocably poisoned and diseased as soon as they are allowed in contact with the colonised race. The custom of colonised people, their traditions, their myths – above all their myths – are the very sign of their poverty of spirit and of their constitutional depravity ... But the triumphant communiques from the missions are, in fact, the source of information concerning the implantation of foreign influences in the core of the colonised people. I speak of the Christian religion, and no-one need be astonished. The Church in the colonies is the white people's Church, the foreignist Church. She does not call the natives to God's ways but to the ways of the white man, of the Master, of the oppressive. And as we know, in this matter many are called but few chosen.[24]

Kamenju's argument is congenial to Ngugi and suggests useful guidelines for looking at the impulse in his novels. Ngugi himself says in an interview that his work is very closely in tune with that, not only of p'Bitek, but also of Leonard Kibera, Charles Mangua and one or two others writing in East Africa at present. The force of the statements extrapolated by Kamenju from Fanon apply not only to *A Grain of Wheat* and *Petals of Blood* (novels written after Ngugi is said to have been introduced to Fanon), but to *The River Between, Weep Not, Child* and to some of the short stories as well. The connection between the latter two novels and Fanon's prescriptions are plain when one considers this statement from *The Wretched of the Earth*:

> In the colonial countries, the spirit of indulgence is dominant at the core of the bourgeoisie; and this is because the national bourgeoisie identifies itself with

the 'Western Bourgeoisie' from who he has learned his lesson' It follows that the western bourgeoisie along its path of negation and decadence without ever having emulated it in its first stages of exploration and invention ... It is already senile before it comes to know the petulance, the fearlessness or the will to succeed of youth.[25]

The manner in which this sort of belief finds its way into the imaginative evocation of Kenya in both *A Grain of Wheat* and *Petals of Blood* can be postponed for the moment. It will be worthwhile, however, here to say something more in a general way about the conclusions reached by Fanon in his two important books, *Black Skin, White Masks* and *The Wretched of the Earth*.

In *Black Skin, White Masks* Fanon examines the socio-economic causes of mental stress within the context of armed revolution. Where Fanon had at first attributed the myth of colour as the main source of racist oppression, he began to see not a psychological aberration but a political phenomenon – colonialism based on technological power – as the real enemy.[26] He determined that his purpose as a psychiatrist was to 'prevent man from feeling a stranger in his own environment' and that in fact this could not achieved by treating the man. It was the environment that had to be changed. In the Algerian war he saw French soldiers and policemen become systematic torturers. He saw Algerians become informers against their own families and comrades. He had both the tortured and the torturers come to him for treatment. He saw the devastating psychological after-effects on both the torturer and the tortured. He saw, that is, how men had to live in their consciences with the recollection of the consequences of their actions.

In *The Wretched of the Earth* Fanon articulates his philosophy of revolution, a philosophy which derives from his experiences of the Algerian struggle and his work as a psychiatrist. He concludes that the colonial victim can only free himself from oppression by a socialist revolution and that the revolution must be achieved by violence. The instrument of the revolution will not be, as in the case of traditional Marxist thinking, the urban proletariat, but the poor peasants – the wretched of the earth. There is both a psychological and political base for the philosophy of *The Wretched of the Earth*. Fanon's medical experience showed him that the victim of colonialist violence could win back his manhood and his emotional wholeness only by using violence himself. He asserts further that what patients needed was not psychiatric treatment but guns in their hands. His disillusionment with the French left-wing parties convinced him, as well, that the notion of the solidarity of the workers of the world was fallacious. He saw that the working classes of the

First and Second World countries profited as much from colonial exploitation as did the ruling classes. Thus, one must turn to the peasantry which has nothing to lose and is the only class uncorrupted by the inculcation of individualistic values – values based on western materialism – to achieve the revolution. Fanon's theories have been challenged by a number of critics who see them as incomplete, or as having in them contradictions. The point is that Fanon, vague as his revolutionary doctrine may be in some respects, is seen as having made an important contribution to social philosophy, a contribution acknowledged by all his critics.

The analogies within Ngugi's work are plain enough. His principal theme is concerned with the legitimate aspirations of the peasantry, from which stock all Kenyans come. Peter Nazareth identifies three specific circumstances which Ngugi treats in the novels: first, the historical setting which deals with the social situation in the round; secondly, the psychological situation of people which he calls a psychological sub-text; and, thirdly, an inquiry into whether 'there is any hope that any of the scarred souls may regain their holds'.

The betrayal of these aspirations of the peasantry, by the creation of a bourgeois class, is the theme of the latest novel. But the inquiry was initiated in the first piece of creative work, *The Black Hermit*, and continues to the point in Ngugi's life where he was arrested for making manifest a vision of this betrayal at the level of peasant understanding, that is, illiterate understanding. Ngugi's Marxism in terms of his presentation of the plight of the peasantry in contemporary Kenya is a straightforward thing. By some commentators it is seen as both naive and out of date. There are peasants: they need to be looked after. And they are betrayed by their own kind, who have assumed station of a new bourgeoisie. The political pattern of the novels is straightforward and repetitive. We see people placed in a context where a leader emerges who can articulate the plight of the generality of people, explain the reasons why circumstances obtain, and then prompt a group of people to action. Following the action where certain gains are made, there is an equal amount of disillusionment and despair. So that none of the novels comes to a satisfactory ending in so far as the ideals which are sought are achieved. There are no easy solutions to the problems. They remain.

Ngugi's strength as a novelist proceeds from the way in which he encrusts his political vision with material derived from his own Kenyan background – the peasant values which are the real values as opposed to those new First World values which are taken on by the blacks who become the leaders in the post-independence circumstance. These are contemptible people so far as Ngugi is concerned because of the way they exploit their own kind and secondly, for their repudiation of the heroes of the revolution who brought about those circumstances in which they are able to act as they do. Thus, Dedan Kimathi is Ngugi's legitimate hero: his vision was straightforward, unflinching, uncompromising, ultimately successful. But now he has been repudiated.

After *Petals of Blood* Ngugi wrote *Ngaahika Ndenda* (I will marry when I choose), the play which brought about his arrest. At least and at last in the production of the Kikuyu play Ngugi seems to have found an answer for a question he raised as far back as 1969 when he said in an interview: 'I have reached a point of crisis; I don't know whether it is worth any longer writing in English . . . The problem is this – I know whom I write about. But whom do I write for?' He has found the medium to convey his message and though he knew all along what he wished to say and on whose behalf he wished to say it, he discovered that the audience for what he had to say was the same as those on whose behalf he spoke.

Ngugi has expressed the same sort of general concerns about the choice of language as the West African writers, but he has not had as much to say as they have. One of the reasons is that the West African writers are

> . . . fed linguistically from below. They are fed by the idiom of speech, the rhythm of speech of the people about whom they are writing. You find that, on the whole, West Africans have been in a lot more contact with the English language than the East Africans. And you find that West Africans have even developed a form of English that is peculiar to the West African scene as the Pidgin English. So that somebody like Chinua Achebe finds it easy when he's portraying a character to fall back on Pidgin English as a form of characteriz-ation. We don't on the whole, have an East African English yet, although it may come into being. So the kind of English we have in East Africa is very much the sort of school English with correct grammar, etc. But maybe in a few years' time in East Africa, there will be a variation of English that can be used as a form or method of characterization. Meanwhile we shall be content merely to capture everything of ordinary life and speech, using the so-called standard English.[27]

But there is more to it than the matter of the way in which a linguistic heritage can be conveyed into English. The value to the writer in terms of his political and his artistic purposes are in danger of being compromised when the writer uses an 'international language'. Ngugi said in an interview just before his arrest:

> The language issue is a slightly different one, although it is related to the novel in the sense that it was in the course of writing the novel [*Petals of Blood*] that I came to be more and more disillusioned with the use of foreign languages to express Kenya's soul or to express the social conditions in Kenya. I think people should express their national aspirations and their national history in the

various national languages of Kenya, including the main national language which is Swahili. But all the other national languages like Gikuyu, Luo, Girima, Kambi, Masai, are part and parcel of our national culture and we should express ourselves fully in those national languages, instead of expressing ourselves in foreign languages like English ... The question of what is international itself needs to be questioned very seriously because there is a tendency of imperialists, capitalists, thinking of their own culture as being international and this includes their languages. Often what they mean by this is that they want their language and culture to hold sway in all those areas under exploitation. What this means is that if you learn a people's language and you adopt their culture you are more likely to see yourself in terms of their world outlook and their aspirations and you are likely to see their system not really as an enemy system but as a friendly system with one or two possible anomalies. So you see that the term 'international' depends upon the base from which you look at it.[28]

One notes the irony of the situation in relation to the question of language that while *Petals of Blood* provoked a good deal of concern among senior officials and minions in the Kenyan government when it was published, suggesting that Ngugi's arrows were finding their marks squarely enough, that that novel was not sufficient to provoke them to the action they took. When a play was written in Gikuyu language, operating at the grass roots in describing circumstances wherein the new élite exploit their own people was made plain, it did provoke officialdom to strike.

One can only speculate on the way in which Ngugi's art will develop in the future. His major achievement as a writer to date has been in English. And his literary models have been for the most part writers in the English tradition. Of these he acknowledges Joseph Conrad and D. H. Lawrence as the most important.

In an interview with Dennis Duerden, Ngugi says that it was from Lawrence he learned to enter 'into the soul of the people and not only of the people but even of the land, of the countryside, of things like plants, of the atmosphere'.[29] And he goes on to say: 'When I am reading D. H. Lawrence, I feel the spirituality of things very near to me as if I am touching the very spirit of things'.[30] He acknowledges, as well, the influence of Conrad by saying that what impressed him with Conrad was the way

he questions things, re-questions things, like action, the morality of action, for instance ... Reading Conrad one feels struck by man's capacity for bearing suffering, but much more than this, he questions what appears on the surface. He questions what I call 'the morality of action'. What is 'success', for instance? What we normally call success? What is, 'action'? Is failure to make a decision, a moral action or not? So you find that some characters in Conrad fail to do something, but their failure to do something has impressed me a lot, because with Conrad I have felt I have come into contact with another whose questioning to me is much more important than the answers which he gives'.[31]

Several commentators – Ben Obumselu, C. P. Sarvan, Ime Ikiddeh and Peter Nazareth – have written articles on Ngugi's debt to Conrad. Peter Nazareth, a close friend and fellow student of Ngugi at Makerere, tells us that Ngugi chose to study Conrad as the 'special subject' while at Makerere and this in itself suggested an affinity of sensibility.[32] Nazareth says that Ngugi learnt a good deal of technique from contemplation of Conrad's writing, a technique which would sustain the affinity of sensibility. Nazareth describes the similarities between *Nostromo*[33] and *A Grain of Wheat*. He refers as well to similarities between *A Grain of Wheat* and Conrad's *Under Western Eyes*.[34] It is not my purpose here to describe the comparisons which Peter Nazareth draws – readers will find them for themselves in his book of essays – but they have to do with structure, with the unifying agency of a more or less central character in the midst of a variety of characters, all of whom might be called central (in *A Grain of Wheat* it is Mugo, in *Nostromo* it is Nostromo, and in *Under Western Eyes* it is Razumov), and with the presence of a variety of levels of irony in the work of each author. Nazareth notes, as well, the comparison between Razumov and Mugo in a general thematic way – both men wish to remain uninvolved with people around them but find once they make an act of serious consequence (in the case of each of them the betrayal of a friend which results in that friend's death), they become more and more involved in affairs, recognize that they have betrayed their own humanity and find that only through confession can they achieve peace of mind, even though this secures their doom.

His absorption of the techniques of the two writers who most influenced him at the outset of his writing career, has helped him to serve his joint purpose as novelist. That is to say, he can wed his public vision to his artistic capacity and produce novels which show how the lives of individuals are given impetus, shape, direction, and area of concern by the social, political and economic forces in the society. The language is that of the *Homecoming* essays, which were written as Ngugi says as an integral part of his fictional world. In an interview given at about the time of the publication of *Petals of Blood*, Ngugi acknowledges again his debt to the neo-romanticism of D.H. Lawrence and the questioning attitude of Joseph Conrad. But he says now that he feels more drawn toward Tolstoy and Zola. He says: 'If I was to start writing all over again, I would write like Zola and not like Lawrence.' The statement is interesting in light of the response of one reviewer in the Nairobi *Sunday Times* to *Petals of Blood* where he says *Petals of Blood* makes 'an addition to the genre of the proletarian novel', and compares Ngugi's achievements to that of Zola. At the same time it was observed by some critics of *Petals of Blood* that the weakness of the novel as a work of the creative imagination lies 'in the author's somewhat dated Marxism: revolt of the masses, elimination of the black Bourgeois; Capitalism to be replaced with African socialism. The author's didacticism weakens what would otherwise have been his finest work'. That is to say, its affinity with such writers as Zola. There is still a good deal more to be said about Ngugi's achievement and the effect of his social thinking on his art; but it would seem that the kind of political solution he proposes while it may be out of date in other countries which have effected the peasant revolutions, is suited still to the landscape of Kenya. It would seem especially true in light of the effect of the play, both in terms of the reaction it prompted from the peasants and workers and from the government.

In my discussion I treat *The River Between* first because it deals with the earliest period of the four novels, the time of the coming of the European into Kenya and dramatizes the circumstances which Ngugi discusses in various prose statements.

Weep Not, Child, the first published novel but the second written, brings Ngugi to his central theme which is the struggle for Kenyan independence and the effect of the struggle on the lives of individuals within the Kenyan context. *Weep Not, Child* is less complex in its form than *A Grain of Wheat*, and less complex still than *Petals of Blood*. But the theme is the same where we find reference to various historical revolutionary activities before the Mau Mau independence movement got under way in the 1950s. In both *Weep Not, Child* and *A Grain of Wheat* the causes and the prosecution of Mau Mau aspirations are dramatized. Introduced at the end of *A Grain of Wheat* is the subject-matter which is to be explored at greater breadth and depth in *Petals of Blood*, a novel almost Victorian in proportion, Ngugi displays present-day Kenya.

REFERENCES AND NOTES

1. Ngugi wa Thiong'o, *Homecoming* (London: Heinemann Educational Books, 1972), p. x.
2. Alan Marcuson, Mike Gonzalez and Dave Williams, 'James Ngugi interviewed by fellow students at Leeds University', CULEA, 31 (1967), p. 2.

3. *Ibid.*
4. Ngugi wa Thiong'o, *Secret Lives* (London: Heinemann Educational Books, first published 1975, reprinted 1979), p. xi.
5. Ngugi wa Thiong'o, *Homecoming, op. cit.*, pp. 149–50.
6. Alan Marcuson, *et al.*, *passim.*
7. Ngugi wa Thiong'o, *Homecoming, op. cit.*, p. xv.
8. *Ibid.*, pp. xvi–xvii.
9. Reinhard Sander and Ian Munro, 'Tolstoy in Africa', *Ba Shiru*, vol. 5 (1973), p. 22.
10. Bette J. Parker, 'BBB interviews Ngugi wa Thiong'o', *Black Books Bulletin*, 6, 1 (Spring 1978), p. 51.
11. Ngugi wa Thiong'o, *Homecoming, op.cit.*, p. 31.
12. *Ibid.*, p. 32.
13. *Ibid.*, p. 34.
14. *Ibid.*, pp. 35–6.
15. 'An interview with Ngugi', *The Weekly Review* (Nairobi: 9 January 1978), p. 10.
16. Ime Ikiddeh, 'Ngugi wa Thiong'o: the novelist as historian', in Bruce King and Kolawole Ogungbesan (eds.), *A Celebration of Black African Writing* (Zaria: Ahmadu Bello University Press; London: OUP, 1975), pp. 204–17.
17. *Ibid.*, p. 204.
18. *Ibid.*
19. 'An interview with Ngugi', *The Weekly Review, op. cit.*
20. Cosmo Pieterse and Donald Munro, *Protest and Conflict in African Literature* (London: Heinemann Educational Books, 1979), p. 62.
21. Peter Nazareth, '*A Grain of Wheat*: a socialist novel?', in *Literature and Society in Modern Africa* (Nairobi: EALB, 1972), p. 128 *et passim.*
22. Grant Kamenju, 'Black aesthetics and pan-African emancipation' (UMMA, III, 2, 1972), p. 57.
23. *Ibid.*
24. *Ibid.*, p. 58.
25. Frantz Fanon, *The Wretched of the Earth* (Penguin Books, 1965), p. 124.
26. Frantz Fanon, *Black Skin, White Masks* (Penguin Books, 1966), p. 108.
27. Reinhard Sander and Ian Moore, *op. cit.*, p. 23.
28. 'An interview with Ngugi', *The Weekly Review, op. cit.*, p. 11.
29. Cosmos Pieterse and Dennis Duerden, *African Writers Talking* (London: Heinemann Educational Books, 1972), p. 123.
30. *Ibid.*
31. *Ibid.*, p. 124
32. Peter Nazareth, *op. cit.*
33. *Ibid.*
34. *Ibid.*

2 *The River Between*

▼▼▼▼▼▼▼▼▼▼▼▼▼▼▼▼▼▼▼▼▼▼▼▼▼▼▼▼▼▼▼▼

Colonialism is not satisfied merely with holding a people in its grip and emptying the native's brain of all form and content. By a kind of perverted logic, it turns to the past of the oppressed people and distorts, disfigures and destroys it ... For colonialism this vast continent was the haunt of savages, a country riddled with superstitions and fanaticism, destined for contempt, weighed down by the curse of God, a country of cannibals – in short, the Negro's country.
Frantz Fanon

*T*HE *RIVER BETWEEN* represents the first phase of Ngugi's artistic recreation of the cultural history of his people. It is a modest beginning in a small novel that dramatizes the antagonism between two rival factions within the same clan, a rivalry which has its origins in promises made to the Gikuyu people in their Creation Myth as the promise is modified in the prophecy of a legendary seer of the tribe. Murungu, the great god, when he created Gikuyu and Mumbi, the original parents of the tribe, told them:

'This land I give to you, O man and woman. It is yours to rule and till, you and your posterity.' (p. 2)

The founding legend is the cornerstone of Ngugi's art, reiterated in each of his novels. His fiction is a systematic fictional examination of the consequences of the alienation of the people from their land, thus effectively from life. Murungu's promise is compromised by the coming of the white man and has been prophesied by Mugo wa Kibiro, a great Gikuyu sage. Mugo has said:

'There shall come a people with clothes like butterflies.' (p. 2)

These were the white men and the novel tells the extent to which the prophecy has been fulfilled. Mugo wa Kibiro was ignored by his people in his own day just as his later-day heir, Chege, has been. Chege, too, has warned the people of the ridges, Makuyu and Kameno, of the arrival of the Europeans. The Europeans have established themselves in Murungu, Nyeri and Kiambu, in Tumu Tumu, in Kikuyu, Limuru and Kijabe. But it is not until the Christian Siriana missionary centre is established that G Chege's people accept the reality of the prophecy.

The novel becomes a dramatic rendering of the consequences of this coming of the white man and in it Ngugi contrives a plot in which to examine a number of related themes – the force of the sense of proprietorship of the land as vested in the Creation Myth of the Gikuyu; the effect of the first coming of European influence in the form of Christian teaching; the attraction of new ideas and interpretation of religious meaning to a group of people ready to receive them; the place and uses of education of the kind provided by the tribe in custom and embodied in ritual and ceremony, and that of a foreign kind as provided by the Christian missionary teachers, of the relation of the Christian missions to the political and military forces which alienate the people from their land. All these things are touched on in the book, though Ngugi's interests are principally three. He examines the divisive influence of the Europeans on he autonomy of the tribe and explores the possibility, first through a consideration of education, and ultimately in an advocacy of love, of reconciling opposite ideas and factions. He senses that the historical process of change displayed in the novel is one which cannot be reversed an yet is not able, it seems, to articulate – or render in terms of art – a view of the historic process wherein a feudal class of people in the grip of superior power and in the sway of new ideas moves through a stage of alienation from the land and from customs and tradition, progressing, ultimately, to the stage reached in the latest novel, *Petals of Blood*, where one sees a culmination of the process in the contending bourgeoise-capitalist and proletariat classes in present-day Kenya.

Ngugi is concerned, then, with the alienation of the people from their rightful inheritance. But he is also interested in the motives of people as they are forced to make moral choices. The book at one level of meaning, and in themes running parallel to the public themes it examines, is a study in individual alienation, as it is in all his fiction writing. Ngugi's control of his materials is not firm enough when he writes this book to provide the sort of examination in terms of theme and character that he will later, in the mature novels, *A Grain of Wheat* and *Petals of Blood*. But the terms of the inquiry are set forth just as are those related to the themes of education and religion.

The main theme of the novel is the conflict between two groups within a single tribe, one of which lives on Makuyu ridge and the other on Kameno. The rivalry has its roots deep in the history of the tribe and is given contemporary focus when European ideas, principally in the form of Christian teaching, find their way into the community. Kameno is the home of traditional cultural values, famous for its association with the founding parents of the tribe, Gikuyu and Mumbi and Mugo wa Kibiro. Chege is the leader of the traditionalists. Descended from Mugo wa Kibiro, he has warned his kinsmen of the advent of the Europeans. But he has failed in prompting them to action and, ignored as was his illustrious forebear, he has withdrawn in his old age from active participation in the affairs of the clan. But Chege knows of the age-old prophecy which says that a saviour will come among the people to rescue them from the invaders. He had hoped in his youth that he might be that figure. His rejection by his people shows him this is not to be and so he places his hopes for fulfilment of the prophecy in his son, Waiyaki, the principal character in the novel:

> 'Now, listen my son. Listen carefully, for this is the ancient prophecy . . . I could not do more. When the white man came and fixed himself in Siriana, I warned all the people. But they laughed at me. Maybe I was hasty. Perhaps I was not the one. Mugo often said you could not cut the butterflies with a panga. You could not spear them until you learnt and knew their ways and movement. Then you could trap, you could fight back. Before he died, he whispered to his son the prophecy, the ancient prophecy: "Salvation shall come from the hills. From the blood that flows in me, I say from the same tree, a son shall rise. And his duty shall be to lead and save the people!" '(p. 20)

Chege is the embodiment of tribal ideology but not so narrowly traditionalist as Kabonyi, who succeeds him on his death. For Chege sees the truth of Mugo's prediction in the presence of the Europeans. And in seeking to prepare Waiyaki for the prophesied role of saviour, he sends the boy to Siriana School (with his boyhood friends Kamau, the son of Kabonyi, and Kinuthia). Waiyaki is to gain an understanding of the white man's ways the better to combat them. Ironically, because Chege fails to see that education does in fact lead one away from familiar ideas and concepts to new and different ones, to new and different peoples and experiences, he sows the seeds of his son's alienation and ultimate destruction.

Makuyu ridge is the seat of clansmen who have adopted Christianity. Their leader is Joshua. Joshua's character is that of the over-zealous, convert to a new ideology. His interpretation of Christianity derives from the Old Testament, from Moses and the Patriarchs – vengeance is his and not the redeeming love of the New Testament. He is fanatical in proselytizing the Christian faith. He demands complete submission to his interpretation of it and condemns all ritual associated with the traditional religion as anathema to God's will. He is particularly repelled by the ceremony of circumcision and, ironically, it is the fact that his own daughter, against his will, participates in the ceremony and loses her life as a result, which brings about the crisis in the novel from which all subsequent events follow.

When Chege dies, Kabonyi becomes the leader of Kameno. An early convert to Christianity with Joshua, Kabonyi has repudiated the religion when he realizes that he will never achieve Joshua's reputation as a preacher. Thus, as much out of motives of jealousy as from a concern for preserving the traditional culture, he founds a secret society, the Kiama, and administers oaths to guarantee allegiance to the ways of the ridges and toward ridding the country 'of the influence of the white man'. Positions are thus taken up and fiercely held as Waiyaki grows to young manhood, passing through his 'second birth', a phase which prepares him for proper initiation into manhood. When Chege dies, Waiyaki assumes the responsibility for his family. As yet he cannot tell if he will be the saviour from the hills as prophesied by the prophet Mugo. But, because of his education at Siriana School and his sense of his place in the legendary history of the people as his father has conveyed it to him, he comes to embody in himself the split between the traditionalists and the Christians. The extent to which his experiences at Siriana have been alienating ones is made plain at the time of his initiation into full manhood. While he participates for a time in the spontaneous frenzy which accompanies and makes tolerable the rite, he is unable to sustain his feeling at being at one with the clan:

> Waiyaki remained where he was standing, feeling slightly dizzy and numb. Gradually he woke from his numbness. He was troubled. He walked back to the crowd. But he now knew that they would not catch him again for he was apart from it all. That night a feeling that he lacked something, that he yearned for something beyond him, came in low waves of sadness that would not let him sleep. (p. 44)

The reasons for this Waiyaki himself knows. His 'absence from the hills had kept him out of touch with those things that most mattered to the tribe' (p. 39). Waiyaki is the victim of his own success.

Waiyaki has lost what Muthoni, the daughter of Joshua, achieves. Muthoni participates in the circumcision ceremony, flying in the face of her father's forbidding, and earning ultimately his curse, because she believes she can be a Christian and yet participate in the traditional life of the tribe.

Muthoni, a baptized Christian, seeks to be:

'A woman made beautiful in the tribe; a husband for my bed; children to play around the hearth ... Yes – I want to be a woman made beautiful in the manner of the tribe.'(p. 44)

Muthoni accepts the Christian message as her father and the missionaries give it to her. But she is confused by the lack of logic she sees in her situation:|

'I want to be a woman. Father and Mother are circumcised. But why are they stopping me, why do they deny me this? How could I be outside the tribe, when all the girls born with me at the same time have left me?' (p. 44)

She senses the way in which her action will be interpreted:

'No one will understand. I say I am a Christian and my father and mother have| followed the new faith. I have not run away from that. But I also want to be initiated into the ways of the tribe. How can I possibly remain as I am now?' (p. 43)

She dies having achieved in her dying delirium her quest of reconciliation:

'Waiyaki', she turned to him, 'tell Nyambura I see Jesus. And I am a woman, beautiful in the tribe ... ' (p. 53)

Muthoni's dying vision is beatific. She proclaims her happiness. In her is embodied the flexibility required by the tribe, the need to adapt to change in order to survive. Ironically her sacrifice is lost on the characters who surround her. Muthoni's death serves only to drive the opposing factions farther apart. For her father, Muthoni ceases to exist:

To Joshua, indulging in this ceremony was the unforgivable sin. Had he not been told to take up everything and leave Egypt? He would journey courageously, a Christian soldier, going on to the promised land. Nobody would deflect him from his set purpose. He wanted to enter the new Jerusalem a whole man.
In fact, Joshua believed circumcision to be so sinful that he devoted a prayer to asking God to forgive him for marrying a woman who had been circumcised.,

God, you know it was not my fault.
God, I could not do otherwise, and she
did this while she was in Egypt. (p. 31)

Her treachery is like that of Lot's wife. Cursed on Earth, she will be cursed in Heaven.

For Livingstone, the head of the mission, her ugly death, the brutal mutilation of her body, confirms the immorality of the Gikuyu:

And then Muthoni died after circumcision – after this brutal mutilation of her body. People would accuse him. He felt cheated by fate. Circumstances were laughing at his old age. But he would show them that the spirit of the Lord still burnt in him. Age did not matter. It was Christ who would be fighting the Prince of Darkness through him, yes, Christ working in him, making him young in action. Circumcision had now to be fought by all means in their hands. He could count on Joshua and Kabonyi to help him. (p. 56)

Though Joshua and Livingstone come to the same conclusions, the intellectual base from which they operate is different. Joshua's reaction is determined by blind faith. Livingstone makes a judgement about the morality of the circumcision ceremony; for him it is a manifestation of moral turpitude and for that reason it must be stamped out.

For Chege, her death is a portent and affirms his reactionary attitudes:

Had he not foreseen this drama? Had he not seen the estrangement between father and daughter, son and father, because of the new faith? This was a punishment to Joshua. It was also a punishment to the hills. It was a warning to all, to stick to the ways of the ridges, to the ancient wisdom of the land, to its ritual and song.
Would Joshua listen? Would Kabonyi hearken to the voice of angry Murungu? Chege feared for them. He feared for those who had embraced strange gods. Would the ridges listen and rise up together? Makuyu was now the home of the Christians while Kameno remained the home of all that was beautiful in the tribe. Who would ever bring them together? (p. 54)

But Muthoni's death provided Waiyaki with a purpose. He had come to view his father's belief that he would fulfil the ancient prophecy 'mainly as an illusion, an old man's dream' (p. 39), yet Muthoni's attempt to reconcile traditional beliefs in Christianity has helped to define his purpose. Now banned from Siriana because he has been initiated into the clan, Waiyaki opens an independent school and eventually organizes many more schools throughout the area. His purpose is to reunite the tribe and to do this through education. He achieves considerable success and popularity. Ultimately he becomes a revered and powerful figure in the tribe and thus engenders the fear and hatred of Kabonyi and his son Kamau.

Kabonyi is the only other person on the ridges who knows of the prophecy of Mugo wa Kibiro and in his youth he, like Chege, hoped he might be the promised saviour. When he recognizes he is not he does not retire like Chege but works hard to win power in the clan. Moreover, he has hopes for his son Kamau similar to those of Chege for Waiyaki.

A second consequence of Muthoni's death is to bring Waiyaki into touch with Nyambura, Muthoni's sister, with whom he falls in love. And in his love for Nyambura, Waiyaki sows the seeds of his own and her destruction. They come to see that a union between them is essential as well as inevitable to their personal happiness even though they recognize marriage would bring down the wrath of both Joshua and Kabonyi on their heads – she is uncircumcised and thus unacceptable to the Kiama; he is circumcised and thus abominated by Joshua.

The climax to the novel comes when Waiyaki is denounced by the Kiama for having attended a Christian service (not for the purpose of hearing the Christian message, but for the chance it affords of seeing Nyambura), and later for warning Joshua that violence is planned against the Christians by the followers of Kabonyi. Waiyaki is challenged by Kabonyi to repudiate his love for Nyambura. And when he cannot they are both passed over to the Kiama for trial and, presumably, for execution.

In dramatizing Waiyaki's attempt to fulfil the prophecy of Mugo wa Kibiro Ngugi makes the first tentative probings into a question which will concern him more and more in his writings – the implications of the imposition of an education system, thus by implication European cultural norms, on the African peasantry. In the novel Kabonyi asks what Waiyaki wants to do, what he wants the people to do with the formal education he is so zealous to cultivate. Kabonyi asks the rhetorical question – 'Do you think the education of the tribe, the education and wisdom which you all received, is any way below that of the white man?' (p. 95). Kabonyi sees more plainly than Waiyaki (and Chege before him) the dangers inherent in taking on the ways of the white man which Waiyaki's school provides. For all of its independence status Waiyaki's school teaches what he has learned at Siriana. Kabonyi sees, albeit in simplistic terms, that to follow Waiyaki is to widen the gap that already exists in the tribe by adding, in general terms, an alien culture to the alien religion.

Neither Waiyaki (nor Ngugi at this point) can give specific answers to Kabonyi's questions. Ngugi here paints himself into a corner. He finds himself with a hero whom he in many ways admires, espousing causes about which he has reservations. This probably accounts for the perpetration of the least convincing scene in the novel, the description of Waiyaki's response to Kabonyi's specific charges:

Kabonyi had touched on a sore spot, the question of youth. When Waiyaki stood up again the old defiance came back. The courage that had made him famous among the boys of his *riika* was now with him. At first he just looked at the people and held them with his eyes. Then he opened his mouth and began to speak. And his voice was like the voice of his father – no – it was like the voice of the great Gikuyus of old. Here again was the saviour, the ones whose words touched the souls of the people. People listened and their hearts moved with the vibration of his voice. And he, like a shepherd speaking to his flock, avoided any words that might be insulting. In any case, how could he repudiate Kabonyi's argument? Waiyaki told them that he was their son. They *all* were his parents. He did not want to lead. The elders were there to guide and lead the youth. And youth had to listen. It had to be led in the paths of wisdom. He, Waiyaki, would listen. All he wanted was to serve the ridges, to serve the hills. They could not stand aloof. They could never now remain isolated. Unless the people heeded his words and plans, the ridges would lose their former dignity and would be left a distance behind by the country beyond . . . (p. 96)

But we do not hear his words nor learn of his plans and so have no notion as to why the people follow him with grateful hearts.

That Ngugi is at best vague on the subject likely explains why the theme of education eventually peters out. Waiyaki's uncertainty and vagueness about the kind of education he would provide and its purposes, is matched by his political naivety. Waiyaki is determined that unity in the clan is necessary for two reasons: first, because the rent between Joshua and Kabonyi was widening and the antagonism becoming more shrill, and secondly, because: 'The white people were now pouring into the interior in greater and greater numbers. Indian traders too had come and were beginning to carry on a thriving business' (p. 110). But Waiyaki never equates the abstractions of his dream of education with the means of making it practical:

> For Waiyaki the fleeting feeling of guilt at having failed to preach reconciliation was now growing stronger. He had missed the opportunity at a time when he could have made his stand clear. A combination of events, excitement and Kabonyi had made him lose that moment when he had the people from the various ridges under control. Would such a chance come again? (p. 110)

Kinuthia, Waiyaki's boyhood friend and a teacher at his school, has a better perception about how schooling may be used than Waiyaki and though the terms of his argument are vague, they are less vague than Waiyaki's:

> Kinuthia was moved not so much by the words as by the way in which Waiyaki said them. There was fire and conviction in them. Yet he wondered if Waiyaki knew that people wanted action now, that the new enthusiasm and awareness embraced more than the mere desire for learning. People wanted to move forward. They could not do so as long as their lands were taken, as long as their children were forced to work in the settled ridges, as long as their women and men were forced to pay hut-tax. He did not want to tell this now, but he would tell him. One day. For Kinuthia was convinced that Waiyaki was the best man to lead people, not only to a new light through education, but also to new opportunities and areas of self-expression through political independence. Waiyaki was the best man to lead the Kiama. Even now his spirit was responsible for the power the Kiama and Kabonyi exercised on the people. Did Waiyaki know this? As Kinuthia beheld the fire in the Teacher's eyes, he wondered if the vision of a new light had not blinded him. But he believed in him and he wanted to share in this vision and share in the task of its fulfilment. (p. 118)

The connection between education and the political views brought about by contact with the Europeans, the political take-over of Gikuyu lands which Kinuthia mentions is a theme which Ngugi leaves for the most part undeveloped in the novel. There is a hint that he might pursue the theme in Joshua's musings on the rumours that white men were establishing government buildings and beginning to levy taxes on the people. And though the issue is a political one, Joshua is more interested in pondering on it than Waiyaki. Joshua, who knows his Bible well, in adopting the stand he does participate in easing the way for the aliens. Though castigated by his people, Joshua shrugs off their anger:

> He himself knew what a government was, having learnt about this from Livingstone. He knew it was his duty as a Christian to obey the Government, giving unto Caesar the things that are Caesar's and to God the things that are God's. That was what he wanted every Christian to do. And was the white man not his brother? (pp. 31–2)

Waiyaki does not see until too late that his desire to reconcile Joshua and Kabonyi has a political dimension. Seeking not to be identified with either group (indeed, because he has been circumcised he is unacceptable to the Christians), he resigns from the Kiama before whom he had sworn 'an oath of allegiance to the Purity and Togetherness of the tribe' (p. 98) and fails to recognize the strength it gains under Kabonyi's leadership as a result of his abnegation. Kinuthia, politically aware in a way Waiyaki is not, warns his friend:

> 'Be careful, Waiyaki. You know the people look up to you. You are the symbol of the tribe, born again with all its purity. They adore you. They worship you. You do not know about the new oath. You have been too busy. But they are taking the new oath in your name. In the name of the Teacher and the purity of the tribe. And remember Kabonyi hates, hates you. He would kill you if he could. And he is the one who is doing all this. Why? The Kiama has power. Power. And your name is in it, giving it even greater power. Your name will be your ruin. Be careful . . .' (p. 112)

The extent to which Waiyaki's dream of reconciliation is inappropriate is revealed by the fact that it is in the Kiama where one finds the seeds of the legitimate independence movement:

> At home the Kiama was getting more and more power over the people. The cry that started the new schools was again taken up. Keep the tribe pure. And people listened to them because they did not want the tribe to die. And the Kiama wanted to fight for the land which had now been taken by the settler, the missionary and the government. Kabonyi and his followers went from ridge to ridge, getting people to take the oath of allegiance to the purity of the tribe. (p. 109)

Ngugi is irresolute in his treatment here – his heart is with Waiyaki as he preaches a dream of reconciliation based on the education that he can provide and the example he can set. Waiyaki, as we have seen, has few specific answers to important questions and makes a series of foolish miscalculations (a reflection, perhaps, that Ngugi is not wholly at ease in his plotting), which bring about his martyrdom.

The themes of unity and reconciliation in the public sector gradually fade away and are replaced by the story of the growing love between Waiyaki and Nyambura. Here Ngugi explores the theme which most interests him in this novel – the place of love as a means of achieving personal redemption and by extension as an agent for redemption in the community. The love between Waiyaki and Nyambura has, as we have noted, its beginnings in the death of Muthoni. We recall that Muthoni's death has, ironically, prompted not reconciliation but a polarization of antagonisms in the clan. The issue is the right of circumcision – an abomination for the Christians, and affirmation of traditional values for the tribe. And it is against this antagonism that the relationship of Nyambura and Waiyaki grows. In their love they find a recognition of the reconciliation Muthoni's death implies. Reflecting on her sister's motives which culminated in her death:

> Nyambura knew then that she could never be saved by Christ; that the Christ who died could only be meaningful if Waikayi was there for her to touch, for her to feel and talk to. She could only be saved through Waiyaki. Waiyaki then was her Saviour, her black Messiah, the promised one who would come and lead her into the light.
>
> Muthoni said she had seen Jesus. She had done so by going back to the tribe, by marrying the rituals of the tribe with Christ. And she had seen Him through suffering. She had been circumcised and said she had become a woman. Nyambura too wanted to become a woman but she could only be so if Waiyaki talked to her, if he stood near her. Then she would see Christ. (p. 103)

Nyambura re-enacts her sister's spiritual quest. Like Muthoni she accepts the brand of Christianity Joshua preaches, partly out of fear of him but partly because it seems to fulfil her spiritual need. But the example of Muthoni, the fact that she achieved peace even in death causes Nyambura to seek some resolution to the conflict which comes to divide her – her loyalty to her father and his religion, and her own spiritual needs. In a long passage, redolent with biblical associations, Nyambura reflects on her need for spiritual consolation and Waiyaki's place in her life:

> Day by day she became weary of Joshua's brand of religion. Was she too becoming a rebel? No. She would not do as her sister had done. She knew,

however, that she had to have a God who would give her a fullness of life, a God who would still her restless soul; so she clung to Christ because He had died on the Tree, love for all the people blazing out from His sad eyes. She wished He could be near her so that she might wash and dress His wounds. She envied Mary, the Mary who had anointed the feet of Christ with oil. She prayed to Him. He must not leave her. Even this did not always satisfy her and she hungered for somebody human to talk to; somebody whom she could actually touch and feel and not a Christ who died many years ago, a Christ who could only talk to her in the spirit. If only she could meet Waiyaki more often; if only he could stay near her, then Christ would have a bigger meaning for her. But Waiyaki was becoming important and he was on the other side. Perhaps they would remain like that, a big, deep valley separating them. Nyambura knew then that she could never be saved by Christ; that the Christ who died could only be meaningful if Waiyaki was there for her touch, for her to feel and talk to. She could only be saved through Waiyaki. Waiyaki then was her Saviour, her black Messiah, the promised one who would come and lead her into the light. (pp. 102–3)

Nyambura recognizes that Muthoni had seen Jesus and she had married the rituals of the tribe to Christ and that she had seen Him through suffering. Waiyaki, too, sees in Nyambura's example an analogy with his public quest to reunify the clan. Nyambura comes to symbolize his quest for unity. 'He would fight for unity and Nyambura was an integral part of that battle. If he lost Nyambura, he too would be lost. He was fighting for his salvation' (p. 164). The word 'salvation' is vital here in suggesting that the quest is both personal and public in its association with the Messianic role Waiyaki has been appointed to play. Waiyaki comes to a recognition similar to that reached by Nyambura that:

A religion that took no count of people's way of life, a religion that did not recognize spots of beauty and truths in their way of life, was useless. It would not satisfy. It would not be a living experience, a source of life and vitality. It would only maim a man's soul, making him fanatically cling to whatever promised security, otherwise he would be lost. (p. 141)

Waiyaki, an advocate of gradualism, is out of joint with his time. Yet he comes closest to defining what he means by education just before he is called to account by the Kiama. Reflecting on the division in the hills, knowing that antagonism arose over the interpretation of the meaning of circumcision, Waiyaki muses:

Circumcision of women was not important as a physical operation. It was what it did inside a person. It could not be stopped overnight. Patience and, above all, education, was needed. If the white man's religion made you abandon a custom and then did not give you something else of equal value, you became lost. An attempt at resolution of the conflict would only kill you, as it did Muthoni. (p. 142)

It is only after the relationship with Nyambura is established that Waiyaki is able to articulate, even if only in very general terms, the nature of his prophesied mission: 'all at once Waiyaki realized what the ridges wanted. People wanted action now. Now he knew what he would preach if he ever got another chance: education for unity. Unity for political freedom' (p. 143). The irony is that their relationship, which becomes tender and loving, associated with the soft murmurings of the River Honia with its spiritual suggestion of 'cure' and with the moonlight in 'sacred' places, is seen, as was Muthoni's death, to stand in opposition to the community which, as a whole, chooses to continue its ancient rivalry, confirming it in current terms. As with many prophets, like his father before him, but more fiercely, Waiyaki is repudiated by those he seeks to serve.

Too late Waiyaki recognizes that he ought to have developed the political aspect of his proselytizing mission. Called before the Kiama to account for his betrayal of the clan, Waiyaki makes an inspired speech recalling the legendary times of the clan, the unity of purpose it possessed and the strength which derived from that unity. But this cannot save him from the denunciation of Kabonyi and Kamau. He is accused of breaking the oath of the Kiama: 'one of the most serious crimes a man could commit. Such a man was doomed to destruction'. Waiyaki, called upon to deny that he will marry Nyambura, that he is Joshua's man because of it, cannot deny his love and conscience:

> Waiyaki stood up and his eyes met those of Nyambura. And he remembered her on this very ground that time she was praying alone; it was the day he first held her in his arms. And she looked beautiful now. She looked like a lamb on the altar of sacrifice. And Waiyaki knew that he could not deny her now, that he could not go back on his love for her. (pp. 150-1)

Personal values - conscience and love - take precedence over expressions of public duty. Love for Nyambura, personal reconciliation, takes precedence over the larger and more difficult issues that the denunciation implies. But the choice is not easy and once again Waiyaki has let the opportunity slip through his grasp:

> And how could he tell them now that he had not betrayed them, that this was not what he meant by unity; that he was not in league with Joshua? How could he tell them that he meant to serve the hills; that he meant to lead them into a political movement that would shake the whole country, that would tell the white man 'Go'! (p. 151)

In the hysteria of the moment he cannot point out to the people the most bitter irony of all - that: 'the oath did not say that he should not love' (p. 151).

Nyambura and Waiyaki are turned over to the Kiama, for judgement and presumably execution. In their deaths is seen a variant re-enactment of Muthoni's death. In their deaths Ngugi seems to imply that ultimately selfless love is the true reconciling agent. The larger public issues remain. The people steal from the ridges quickly in the darkness, not wanting to accept their guilt for the betrayal of the Teacher and Nyambura, perhaps recognizing, but unwilling to admit, what Waiyaki knew – that they have been duped by Kabonyi:

> Neither did they want to speak to one another, for they knew full well what they had done to Waiyaki and yet they did not want to know. (p. 152)

In such circumstances people look for scapegoats, for someone else to blame for their own sins.

Ngugi never fully reconciles contradictions in conception and plot in the novel. He conveys a clear and simplified picture of how a traditional society experiences and reacts to change as alien ideas are imposed on and often adopted by an indigenous culture which is, in part, ready for change. He creates characters who exemplify or symbolize various points of view and yet are convincing enough as human figures, possessing and displaying, again in simplified form, a range of emotions that are compelling. But Ngugi never resolves the question of what education can do in the context to ally animosities. His examination of sacrificial love as an agent of reconciliation is equally unsatisfying. The problem centres in the character of Waiyaki and in the associations which are suggested between him and Christ, within the context of the correspondence between the creation myth of Gikuyu and Mumbi, Adam and Eve, in terms of the Messianic role Chege has urged on Waiyaki. Waiyaki on the one hand cannot clearly define what his role is actually to be and, on the other, is almost self-indulgent in his contemplation of it. The force of the emotional appeal –

> the element of love and sacrifice agreed with his own temperament. The suffering of Christ in the Garden of Gethsemane and His agony on the tree had always moved him. (p. 100)

– is juxtaposed by the uncertainty of the actual role he will serve:

> They called him a saviour. His own father had talked of a Messiah to come. Whom was the Messiah coming to save? From what? And where would He lead the people? Although Waiyaki did not stop to get clear answers to those questions, he increasingly saw himself as the one who would lead the tribe to the light. (p. 101)

This sort of vagueness is typical of Waiyaki and it is hard to accept someone who makes as many blatantly foolish miscalculations and errors in judgement as he does. Not only can he not define what it is he means by the phrase 'education is life' but he seems not to know with any certainty what his commitment to reconciliation really means. Otherwise why would he fail to preach about it when he has the opportunity and why would he take the oath to the Kiama which *de facto* is a declaration for the traditionalist and against the Christian? How is it possible he would not see such an act would make a happy union with Nyambura impossible, and why would he surrender his membership in the Kiama to Kamau, someone he dislikes and has reason to fear? Too late he recognizes his miscalculations. But this makes him a hero in an absurdist drama and not a tragic or even potentially tragic figure.

Waiyaki achieves a martyrdom as the book closes. The formality of the ending matches the formality with which the book opens. And this formality is reflected in the care Ngugi uses in balancing character and theme within the plot, in the simplicity in the syntax and phrasing he adopts in telling his tale. The story has the simplicity of structure, incident and language generally associated with myth and legend. Waiyaki is part of the legend of his people and Ngugi presents him in folk-heroic terms by exploiting similarities between the role he is assigned to play as saviour with that of the biblical Christ, against a legendary history which reveals a strong association between the Gikuyu and the Christian creation myths. Ngugi uses anthropological details sparingly, here and elsewhere in his writing, in rendering the myths of the Gikuyu and in descriptions and dramatizations of rituals and ceremonies. As well as describing the myths associated with Gikuyu and Mumbi, he talks of the legendary figures of Mugo wa Kibiro and Demi na Mathathi. His use of such material is deft and such anthropological detail as he does employ is there not for its own sake but to confirm the meaning of the symbolic world he establishes. He enhances the effect of his book by establishing a pattern of symbols – again used sparingly – which associates people with the land and elaborates their emotional state. The most obvious of these symbols is the designation of the ridges of Makuyu and Kamano which are associated with sleeping lions and the River Honia which is associated with the ceremonial rites of the Christians and the traditionalists. Seen from the valley 'the ridges appear antagonistic'. The antagonism between them is associated with the antagonism between the two parts of the clan. But seen from the mountain top where Waiyaki travels with Chege they 'merge into one area of beautiful land'. In this figure Ngugi suggests the reconciliation which Waiyaki will attempt to achieve.

The second most obvious symbol is the River Honia which Ngugi imbues with a number of ambiguous and ironic associations. For the traditionalists and Christians alike it is the site of the initiation rites – of circumcision and of baptism, each act possessing a symbolic value of its own, a celebration of life. Because of this, it provokes further antagonism. Moreover, the word 'Honia' means 'cure' or 'will to live'. Yet where it should unite it divides, even though the healing power of the river is necessary to each element in the clan, and to Waiyaki and Nyambura in moments of disconsolate musing.

The purification associated with the river, with water, both when it is used for specific ceremonies and at those times when Waiyaki and Nyambura seek consolation from its soft murmurings, is attributed also to the rain, which not only bathes the parched land, but acts as a blessing which staves off possible famine. Ngugi adumbrates a wider meaning to the rain as he associates it, gathering in streams on the ridges, with the image of the lions no longer sleeping but 'crying, crying, for the soil', an expression of fear over the encroachment of the white man in the land. The land is life to the people, and the moods of the characters in the novel are seen in association with the land. For example, 'the peas and beans, bursting into life, gave gay colour and youth to the land' and we learn that 'at such times women could be seen in their shambas cultivating; no, not cultivating, but talking in a secret language with the crops and the soil' (p. 79).

The word 'butterflies' used to describe the white man, with its humorous association, may or may not be a just epithet, but it affords Ngugi with the chance to strike off one of the most telling metaphors in the book. Chege, advising Waiyaki to acquire a European education so he can combat European ways, quotes Mugo, the sage, as saying 'you could not cut butterflies with a panga. You could not spear them until you learnt and knew their ways and movements' (p. 20).

In another mood, the perfection of the love of Nyambura and Waiyaki is associated with moonlight, away from the villages, 'untainted with religion, social conventions or any tradition'. They achieve for a moment perfect serenity and Nyambura becomes the embodiment of feminine beauty, 'symbolized by the flooding movement and the peace around'. Such spots of time pass quickly but Ngugi isolates the moment in the flood of moonlight.

Sometimes the attempt at composing a relevant symbolism goes astray as when it is suggested, as Waiyaki travels the ridges alerting the people to the need for education, that 'the trees, the birds, and the paths he trod, all knew him, knew a man destined to serve his country' (p. 67).

One final comment on the stylistic achievement of the novel. After being told that Kabonyi (and one presumes other of the principal characters in the novel) 'could speak in proverbs and riddles, – [that] nothing could appeal more to the elders, who still appreciated a subtle proverb and witty riddles' (p. 95), it is disappointing to discover that little if any of this sort of material is in the book. Ngugi has not taken the chance he affords himself to secure the authenticity of the people and period he presents by drawing on just this sort of verbal material if, indeed, it exists. We see occasionally single instances when Ngugi uses a telling image as when we are told that Waiyaki's fame 'spread like a fire in a dry brush' or that to his jealous friend Kamau, Waiyaki appears as 'the hawk that always snatched his piece of meat'. But this is not typical of the writing.

With the formality of the design of the book, the neatness of the pattern is a diffidence which makes for a kind of overall vagueness. Ngugi is not able to orchestrate fully the rich complexities of thematic and human relationships the various elements of the plot suggest. None of his characters is able wholly to articulate what he stands for except Joshua who comes perilously close to comic caricature. We know what characters stand for but none of them examines his position at any depth; none seems capable of complex rationalizing or statement either in his private thoughts or public discussion. Moreover, the context in which the antagonism between the clans takes place, the social structure, the religious and political organization of the tribe is never displayed. There are many references to the spiritual basis of the tribe in such phrases as 'being beautiful in the tribe', 'the secrets of the tribe', 'the secret of the hills', 'the ancient wisdom of the land'. This is the language of myth but more than this is needed in a novel which seeks to deal realistically with the central problem the book describes is to be convincing. The circumcision ceremony is the sole exception to this claim: here we gain a clear perception of the purpose the rite serves and the emotions it releases. But we never come to know what the Kiama actually is, what its prescriptions actually are, for all the ominous doom that is associated with offending its code. Similarly, mention is made to the progressive alienation of the Gikuyu from the land by the white colonists. This is the principal theme of all of Ngugi's writing. Yet it is little more than a *leitmotif* in this book.

In *The River Between*, Ngugi lays down the pattern of related forces – social, religious and political – which will concern him in subsequent writing. As he explores the complexity of relationships provided by the historical encounter between Europe and Africa seen over a fifty-year period, he develops a complexity of style compatible with his understanding.

3 *Weep Not, Child*

▼▼▼▼▼▼▼▼▼▼▼▼▼▼▼▼▼▼▼▼▼▼▼▼▼▼▼▼▼▼▼▼▼▼

... [D]ecolonization is always a violent phenomenon ... Its unusual
importance is that it constitutes, from the very first day, the
minimum demands of the colonized. To tell the truth, the proof of
success lies in a whole social structure being changed from the
bottom up. The extraordinary importance of this change is that it is
willed, called for; demanded. The need for this change exists in its
crude state, impetuous and compelling, in the consciousness and in
the lives of the men and women who are colonized. But the
possibility of this change is equally experienced in the form of a
terrifying future in the consciousness of another 'species' of men and
women: the colonizers. *Frantz Fanon*

*W*EEP NOT, CHILD, Ngugi's first published novel, belongs in
subject-matter to the period shortly after the close of the
Second World War when nationalist sentiments came to a
head in Kenya. The events those sentiments provoked, culminating in the
Mau Mau emergency, are seen as they influence the lives of the family of
Ngotho and, though less fully elaborated, the families of Howlands, a
white settler-farmer, and Jacobo, a Kenyan landowner. The events the
novel describes are seen principally from the point of view of Njoroge, the
youngest son of Ngotho, from the time he enters school to a point in the
midst of the emergency, some twelve years later, when, disillusioned by
the destruction of his family, denied the education by which he sought to
fulfil himself and enrich the life of his family and his country, he tries to
take his life.

The novel reveals how all the members of Ngotho's family – his sons
Boro, Kori and Kamau by his wife Njeri and Njoroge by Nyokabi –
become involved in the crisis and suffer the violence it provokes.
Through these experiences Ngugi examines three separate but related
themes: first, the appropriateness of a young Kenyan getting a western
education, secondly, the influence of Christianity in the Kenyan context

(since the education is provided by a mission school) and thirdly, the causes and prosecution of the independence struggle. Ngugi treats this material in a straightforward manner and his examination of the three themes runs more or less parallel, mingling in the life of Njoroge, whose progress in the various schools he attends takes place as the political situation in Kenya deteriorates to the point where Jomo Kenyatta, the political leader of the nationalists, is arrested, tried, found guilty and imprisoned. At the same time a state of emergency is declared, sides in the struggle are drawn up, a number of Kenyans, among them Njoroge's older brothers, Boro and Kori, go into the forest to become freedom fighters. Poised against them are British forces, joined by white farmers who are sworn in as political officers in the emergency, and by Kenyan constabulary. Violence and atrocities are committed on both sides as Mau Mau soldiers seek to drive Europeans from the land from which they have alienated Africans, a land by legend, law and custom rightfully theirs.

The land was given to the Gikuyu people at the time of the creation of the earth, of Gikuyu and Mumbi the archetypal forebears of the Gikuyu. Ngugi discusses the creation thus:

> . . . There was wind and rain. And there was also thunder and terrible lightning. The earth and the forest around Kerinyaga shook. The animals of the forest whom the Creator had recently put there were afraid. There was no sunlight. This went on for many days so that the whole land was in darkness. Because the animals could not move, they just sat and moaned with the wind. The plants and trees remained dumb. It was, our elders tell us, all dead except for the thunder, a violence that seemed to strangle life. It was this dark night whose depth you could not measure, not you or I can conceive of its solid blackness, which would not let the sun pierce through it.
>
> But in this darkness, at the foot of Kerinyaga, a tree rose. At first it was a small tree and grew up, finding a way even through the darkness. It wanted to reach the light, and the sun. This tree had *Life*. It went up, up, sending for the the rich warmth of a blossoming tree – you know a holy tree in the dark night of thunder and moaning. This was Mukuyu, God's tree. Now, you know that at the beginning of things there was only one man (Gikuyu) and one woman (Mumbi). It was under this Mukuyu that he first put them. And immediately the sun rose, and the dark night melted away. The sun shone with a warmth that gave life and activity to all things. The wind and lightning and thunder stopped. The animals stopped wondering and moved. They no longer moaned but gave homage to the Creator and Gikuyu and Mumbi. And the Creator who is also called Murungu took Gikuyu and Mumbi from his holy mountain. He took them to the country of ridges near Siriana and there stood them on a big ridge before he finally took them to Mukuruwe wa Gathanga about which you have heard so much. But he had shown them all the land – yes, children, God showed Gikuyu and Mumbi all the land and told them,
>
> 'This land I hand over to you. O man and woman

It's yours to rule and till in serenity sacrificing
Only to me, your God, under my sacred tree. . . ' (pp. 23–4)

Ngugi conveys two fundamental things in this passage. The land is the source of life to the Gikuyu because it provides food. As important as the material needs it supplies, is the spiritual needs it satisfies. Jomo Kenyatta describes the Gikuyu belief in this way:

Communion with the ancestral spirits is perpetuated through contact with the soil in which the ancestors of the tribe lie buried. The Gikuyu consider the earth as the 'mother' of the tribe, for the reason that the mother bears her burden for about eight or nine moons while the child is in her womb, and then for a short period of suckling. But it is the soil that feeds the child through a lifetime; and again after death it is the soil that nurses the spirit of the dead for eternity. Thus the earth is the most sacred thing above all that dwell in or on it. Among the Gikuyu the soil is especially honoured, and an everlasting oath is to swear by the earth.[1]

Kenyatta writes further in *Facing Mount Kenya* that 'a culture has no meaning apart from the social organization of life on which it is built'.[2] He refers to the systematic alienation of the land by the British, which was conducted by the British dating from 1902. Ime Ikiddeh discusses the history of British intervention in Kenya in these terms:

From the attempt by Joseph Chamberlain in 1902 to found , 'a national home for the Jewish race' on thousands of square miles of land in Kenya and the official appropriation for British ex-soldiers after the World War, to the open seizure and illegal speculation by white settler-farmers that went on all the time, the record of British usurpation of land in Kenya must be one of the most sordid scandals in colonial history.

'The Crown Lands Ordinance of 1902 and subsequent laws in 1915 and after, far from controlling land dealings, led, in fact, to more profitable speculation by Europeans and greater loss to the African population.'

'What individual settlers could own – and before 1902 they could have it for nothing – is illustrated by the case of Lord Delamere, the one-time indomitable leader of the Europeans in Kenya. In 1903 he applied for 156 square miles of leasehold at ½d (pence) per acre, to be held for ninety-nine years with the right of purchasing it permanently at 8d (pence) per acre. Delamere, who already held large tracts of land, was granted 100,000 acres on lease. Such was the rush to acquire land that the Land Commission reported in 1905 that 200% of Masai grazing grounds had been applied for. Forced labour, which included the indiscriminate use of women and children went hand in hand with land, and so did increase in the taxes extracted from the 'natives' . . . Further Land Commissions were set up between 1928 and 1934, but the situation was not much better when Kenyatta returned to his country (in 1946) . . . [3]

The effect of this alienation process is described by Kenyatta in these terms:

When the European comes to the Gikuyu country and robs the people of their land, he is taking away not only their livelihood, but the material symbol that holds family and tribe together.[4]

Weep Not, Child is the artistic expression of the truth of this assertion. Ngotho works on land, once the ancestral land of his forebears, now owned by Howlands, and he lives on land, again once his but now owned by Jacobo. Ngotho acquiesces to his circumstances because he is confident that the prophecy of the Gikuyu sage, Mugo wa Kibiro, that the land will be returned to its rightful owners, will be fulfilled. He believes this despite the experience of dealings he has had with whites and the example his father who, too, had trusted in the prophecy:

'Then came the war. It was the first big war. I was then young, a mere boy, although circumcised. All of us were taken by the force. We made roads and cleared the forest to make it possible for the warring white men to move more quickly. The war ended. We were all tired. We came home worn out but very ready for whatever the British might give us as a reward. But more than this, we wanted to go back to the soil and court it to yield, to create, not to destroy. But Ng'o! The land was gone. My father and many others had been moved from our ancestral lands. He died lonely, a poor man waiting for the white man to go. Mugo had said this would come to be. The white man did not go and he died a *Muhoi* on this very land.' (p. 25)

Boro and Kori have been to war for the British, too. They have seen a brother, Mwangi, Njoroge's older brother die in an alien cause on alien soil. But they draw different conclusions from their experiences of fighting in Egypt, Jerusalem and Burma. They have met members of other 'subject races' who have had similar experiences to their own, and have learned of movements in other parts of the world to repossess land taken from its hereditary owners by imperial conquest. Boro and Kamau can be taken to stand for that generation of Kenyans who were moved to fight for the land when all other forms of appeal were suppressed, often violently. They prefigure Kihika in *A Grain of Wheat*, symbolic of figures who, frustrated by having no land to work, by having fought for little gain in an alien war, take to the forests and affect the return of the land to the rightful owners. They realize that passive waiting will not win them back the land. Moreover, Boro's anger with the status accorded his people by the British spills over on his father. Ngugi presents the situation in plain terms:

Boro thought of his father who had fought in the war only to be dispossessed. He too had gone to war, against Hitler. He had gone to Egypt, Jerusalem and Burma. He had seen things. He had often escaped death narrowly. But the thing he could not forget was the death of his stepbrother, Mwangi. For whom or for what had *he* died?

When the war had come to an end, Boro had come home, no longer a boy but a man with experience and ideas, only to find that for him there was to be no employment. There was no land on which he could settle, even if he had been able to do so. As he listened to this story, all these things came into his mind with a growing anger. How could these people have let the white man occupy the land without acting? And what was all this superstitious belief in a prophecy?

In a whisper that sounded like a shout, he said, 'To hell with prophecy.'

Yes, this was nothing more than a whisper. To his father, he said, 'How can you continue working for a man who has taken your land? How can you go on serving him?'

He walked out, without waiting for an answer. (p. 26)

The anger Boro expresses for his father is the first rent in the 'feeling of oneness [which] most distinguished Ngotho's household from many other polygamous families'. This, Ngugi tells us, 'was attributed to Ngotho, the centre of the home'. The breakup of the home, which the novel dramatizes from this point forward – and the breakup of the homes of Howlands and Jacobo, a comparison which Ngugi sustains to good artistic effect – becomes a metaphor for the breakup of Kenyan society, preparing the way for it to be replaced by a new order, a process not completed by the novel's close and with no suggestion of what the new order might be.

Ngotho continues to work the land for Howlands. Boro and Kori go to work in Nairobi and become involved in the independence movement. Howlands' whole life is in the land. Although his family is about the same size as Ngotho's we learn little of them except that his wife after an initial romantic response to Africa comes to find life almost intolerable and spends her time hiring and firing servants in a futile attempt to work out her frustrations. We know that he has a daughter overseas, that he, like Ngotho, has lost a son overseas in the war and that he has another son, Stephen, about Njoroge's age and with whom Njoroge has a fleeting moment of intimate understanding. Howlands has come to Kenya after the First World War. Described as a 'typical Kenya settler':

He was a product of the First World War. After years of security at home, he had been suddenly called to arms and he had gone to the war with the fire of youth that imagines war and glory. But after four years of blood and terrible destruction, like many other young men he was utterly disillusioned by the 'peace'. He had to escape. East Africa was a good place. Here was a big trace of wild country to conquer. (p. 30)

The irony is that Howlands, disillusioned with his own land, dispossesses the Kenyan of his. When Howlands' son, to whom he planned to pass on the land, is killed in the Second World War his reaction is to turn wholly to the land:

> Mr Howlands lost all faith – even the few shreds that had begun to return. He would again have destroyed himself, but again his god, land, came to the rescue. He turned all his efforts and energy into it. He seemed to worship the soil. (p. 31)

It is in this scene with Howlands, when Ngugi reveals most clearly the irony arising out of the parallel lines their lives have followed. For just as Howlands would have no idea that Ngotho might experience guilt comparable to his own at the loss of a son, so Howlands would have no idea of the force of the idea which binds Ngotho to the land and, ironically draws from Howlands feelings amounting to affection:

> Not that Mr Howlands stopped to analyse his feelings towards him. He just loved to see Ngotho working in the farm; the way the old man touched the soil, almost fondling, and the way he tended the young tea plants as if they were his own ... Ngotho was too much of a part of the farm to be separated from it. (pp. 29–30)

This scene carries a weight of foreshadowing. It is here that Ngotho is disarmed of his view that Howlands will leave the land to return to its hereditary owners, that the prophecy of Mugo wa Kibero will be fulfilled:

> Ngotho's heart jumped. He too was thinking of his children. Would the prophecy be fulfilled soon?
> *'Kwa nini Bwana.* Are you going back to – ? 'No,' Mr Howlands said, unnecessarily loudly.
> ' ... Your home, home ...'
> 'My home is here!'
> Ngotho was puzzled. Would these people never go? But had not the old Gikuyu seer said that they would eventually return the way they had come? And Mr Howlands was thinking, would Stephen really *do*? He was not like the other one. He felt the hurt and the pain of loss. (p. 32)

Shortly after this Ngotho attends a meeting, organized by Boro, Kori and others, to organize a strike. Kiarie, one of the organizers, reminds the crowd of people of their history under colonialism, of their alienation from the land. His speech ends in the familiar pleas of Moses to Pharaoh: 'Let my People go', noting the association between Moses and Jomo, the Black Moses, sent by God to liberate the Kenyan people.

But when Jacobo, 'crystallized into a concrete betrayal of the people', is brought in to pacify the people, Ngotho leads a charge against Jacobo, riot police break up the meeting and the strike fails.

Jacobo is the fourth representative figure in the novel. Howlands, when the emergency is in effect, enunciates a policy of divide and rule –

get the blacks to fight each other and the white man will be safe. But in
fact a policy such as this has been in effect for a long while before the
emergency. Jacobo represents that small number of Africans who were
allowed to own and farm land, who were thus able to accumulate wealth.
But their position depended on the goodwill of the whites and thus people
like Jacobo, both pitiable and contemptible, become their toadies. More
than this, such people become agents of division within the African
community. Boro and his peers are in accord about the reasons for
reclaiming the land but lack agreement over how to do this. Jacobo and
those like him (figures whose mentalities we find explored at greater
depth in Ngugi's later writing) help perpetuate this disarray.

Ngotho's action in the strike further alienates him from Boro who
holds his father accountable for the failure. Moreover, it marks the
beginning of the decline of Ngotho and his family.

It is an irony that Ngotho, in a public act of protest against the
victimization of Africans by Africans, prompted by his clear recognition
of the truth of Boro's claims, destroys his sons' cause. But it is equally an
irony that the revolution which Boro mounts to retrieve the land for the
peasantry has the affect of alienating completely the last generation of
genuine African peasantry, symbolized by Ngotho, from the land.

Ngotho's nadir occurs after the ill-fated strike which fails because
Ngotho, recognizing the treacherous behaviour of Jacobo, on impulse
attacks the latter and provokes a riot. He is fired from his job, his
reputation destroyed as he resides, a supplicant, on the farm of Nganga, a
compassionate farmer.

It is against this background of deepening stress that Njoroge grows
from boyhood to adolescence. When the novel opens his mother asks him
'would you like to go to school?' and he holds his breath, fearing she may
withdraw her words. But she does not and we see in a series of vignettes
how Njoroge's schoolboy career progresses, how he persistently does
better than others. At school he makes a close relationship with Mwihaki,
the daughter of Jacobo. And it is at this time, in listening to discussions in
his father's hut about the problems in the country that he begins to
conceive an important mission for himself:

Njoroge listened to his father. He instinctively knew that an indefinable
demand was being made on him, even though he was so young. He knew that
for him education would be the fulfilment of a wider and more significant
vision – a vision that embraced the demand made on him, not only by his father,
but also by his mother, his brothers and even the village. He saw himself
destined for something big, and this made his heart glow. (p. 39)

Njoroge accepts the teaching of the missionaries and his callow mind elaborates a dream compounded of education and Christian teaching, exploiting the analogy between the two religious forces he is submitted to:

His belief in a future for his family and the village rested then not only on a hope for sound education but also on a belief in a God of love and mercy, who long ago walked on this earth with Gikuyu and Mumbi, or Adam and Eve. It did not make much difference that he had come to identify Gikuyu with Adam and Mumbi with Eve. To this God, all men and women were united by one strong bond of brotherhood. And with all this, there was growing up in his heart a feeling that the Gikuyu people, whose land had been taken by white men, were no other than the children of Israel about whom he read in the Bible. (p. 49)

But the dream is stalemated, even as Njoroge, 'now a big boy, almost a young man' . . . and the 'full force of the chaos that had come over the land was just beginning to be clear in his mind' (p. 84). And it is reduced by the false consolations offered out of the Bible to account for the chaos:

'Turn to the Gospel according to St Matthew, Chapter 24, and beginning to read from line 4.'
There was a shuffle of leaves.
'Let's begin to read . . . '
'And Jesus answered and said unto them: Take heed that no man deceive you.
'For many shall come in My name, saying, I am Christ; and shall deceive many.
'And ye shall hear of wars and rumours of wars: see that ye be not troubled: for all these things must come to pass, but the end is not yet.
'For nation shall rise against nation, and kingdom against kingdom: and there shall be famines, and pestilences, and earthquakes, in divers places.
'All these are the beginning of sorrows.
'Then they shall deliver you up to be afflicted, and shall kill you: and ye shall be hated of all nations for My name's sake.
'And then shall many be offended, and shall betray one another, and shall hate one another.
'And many false prophets shall rise, and shall deceive many.
'And because iniquity shall abound, the love of many shall wax cold.
'*But he that shall endure unto the end, the same shall be saved . . .* '
He read on. But when he came to verse 33, he stopped and stared at all the people in the church. Then he raised his voice and went on:
'Verily I say unto you. This generation shall not pass till all these things be fulfilled . . . '
It was as if darkness too had fallen into the building and there was no one to light the way. (p. 90)

It survives the brutal murder by the Christian police of the revivalist, Isaka, who professes his Christian faith singing with the protection of God he needs no pass. He is beaten and shot, almost before the eyes of his young catechists.
But the dream is not really enough to sustain Njoroge. Its weaknesses

are probed by Mwihaki on one of their meetings. All he has is faith and she knows faith is not enough:

> He became serious and a little distant. He was again in his vision.
> 'Our country has great need of us.'
> 'Do you think the country really needs you?'
> 'Yes,' he said rather irritably. Was she doubting him? 'The country needs me. It needs you. And the remnant. We must get together and rebuild the country. That was what your father told me the day I was at your home.'
> 'The country is so dark now,' she whispered to herself.
> 'The sun will rise tomorrow,' he said triumphantly, looking at her as if he would tell her that he would never lose faith, knowing as he did that God had a secret plan.

Mwihaki's disillusionment is juxtaposed to Njoroge's faith. Mwihaki is a foil to Njoroge throughout the novel. She experiences despair as the horror of the emergency spreads over the land. When he expounds his 'vision' to her she retorts angrily, and out of fear:

> 'You are always talking about tomorrow, tomorrow. You are always talking about *the* country and *the* people. What is tomorrow? And what is *the People* and *the Country* to you?' She had suddenly stopped what she had been doing and was looking at him with blazing eyes. Njoroge saw this and was afraid. He did not want to make her angry. He was pained. He looked at her and then at the plain, the country beyond stretching on, on to the distant hills shrouded in the mist. (p. 106)

Njoroge's faith is in his belief that:

> 'If you knew that all your days life will always be like this with blood flowing daily and men dying in the forest, while others daily cry for mercy; if you knew even for one moment that this would go on for ever, then life would be meaningless unless bloodshed and death were a meaning. Surely this darkness and terror will not go on for ever. Surely there will be a sunny day, a warm sweet day after all this tribulation, when we can breathe the warmth and purity of God ... ' (p. 106)

His words offer optimism of a kind and are a reflection of his duty to prepare himself for his role once the troubles have been passed. But Mwihaki has struck a chord of doubt in him and for a moment his faith, couched in vague abstractions, looks threadbare. Moreover, the speech offers an ironic foreshadowing of Njoroge's ultimate disillusionment. So that when the scene between him and Mwihaki is replayed, in mirror fashion, after his torture by Howlands, it is Njoroge who repudiates his vision and pleads with Mwihaki to fly to Uganda with him. And it is she, always realistic in her appraisals, who speaks of duty:

'We better wait. You told me that the sun will rise tomorrow. I think you were right.'

He looked at her tears and wanted to wipe them. She sat there, a lone tree defying the darkness, trying to instil new life into him. But he did not want to live. Not this kind of life. He felt betrayed.

'All that was a dream. We can only live today.'

'Yes. But we have a duty. Our duty to other people is our biggest responsibility as grown men and women.'

'Duty! Duty!' he cried bitterly.

'Yes, I have a duty, for instance, to my mother. Please, dear Njoroge, we cannot leave her at this time when – No! Njoroge. Let's wait for a new day.'

She had conquered. She knew now that she would not submit. But is was hard for her and as she left him she went on weeping, tearing and wringing her heart. The sun was sinking down. Njoroge's last hope had vanished. For the first time he knew that he was in the world all alone without a soul on whom he could lean. The earth went round and round. He saw everything in a mist. Then all of a sudden, he fell on to the ground and cried 'Mwihaki, oh Mwihaki.' (pp. 133-4)

Njoroge, for all his hope, achieves none of the things he sought and much of what he did not – expulsion from school and employment in the shop of an Asian merchant, both humiliating experiences.

Yet the lyrical possibilities of the dream are most profoundly experienced by Njoroge at the secondary school:

Njoroge was often surprised by these missionaries' apparent devotion to their work. One might have thought that teaching was to them life and death. Yet they were white men. They never talked of colour; they never talked down to Africans; and they could work closely, joke, and laugh with their black colleagues who came from different tribes. Njoroge at times wished the whole country was like this. This seemed a little paradise, a paradise where children from all walks of life and of different religious faiths could work together without any consciousness. (p. 115)

Ironically it is at this moment the dream is dealt its death blow. Police officers come to take Njoroge away to his village. Jacobo has been murdered, Ngotho has confessed the crime and Njoroge has been denounced as an oath taker. Ngotho has been castrated and Njoroge is threatened with the same mutilation. Howlands, now a maniacal District Officer, turns the full fury of his hatred against Ngotho for whom he once held a special fondness. Ngotho is the most treacherous of the Gikuyus in his eyes.

Ngugi brings the novel swiftly to a close. Boro comes out of the forest to

kill Howlands but not before he and his father, in one of the genuinely
moving scenes in the novel, have been reconciled:

> 'Forgive me, father – I didn't know – oh, I thought – ' Boro turned his head.
> The words came out flatly, falteringly. 'It's nothing. Ha, ha, ha! You too have
> come back – to laugh at me? Would you laugh at your father? No. Ha! I meant
> only good for you all. I didn't want you to go away – '
>   'I had to fight.'
>   'Oh there – Now – Don't you ever go away again.'
>   'I can't stay. I can't,' Boro cried in a hollow voice. A change came over
> Ngotho. For a time he looked like the man he had been, firm, commanding –
> the centre of his household.
>   'You must.'
>   'No, father. Just forgive me.'
>   Ngotho exerted himself and sat up in bed. He lifted his hand with an effort
> and put it on Boro's head. Boro looked like a child.
>   'All right. Fight well. Turn your eyes to Murungu and Ruriri. Peace to you
> all Ha! What? Njoroge look ... look – to – your – moth – '
>   His eyes were still aglow as he sank back into his bed. For a moment there was
> silence in the hut. Then Boro stood up and whispered, 'I should have come
> earlier ... ' (p. 124)

In a sense the spirit of the family is revived and Ngotho, even in death,
is once again the centre of the home.

Ngugi takes the opportunity, just before Boro kills Howlands, to
examine the circumstances which have converted Howlands from an
introspective farmer who takes more consolation from his work on the
land than in his family, into a brutal killer who only half understands the
forces which sweep round him and who, in the midst of his brutal
behaviour, finds repugnant the system which has cast him in this role:

> He now knew maybe there was no escape. The present that had made him a
> D.O. reflected a past from which he had tried to run away. That past had
> followed him even though he had tried to avoid politics, government, and
> anything else that might remind him of that betrayal. But his son had been
> taken away ... It was no good calling on the name of God for he, Howlands, did
> not believe in God. There was only one God for him – and that was the farm he
> had created, the land he had tamed. And who were these Mau Mau who were
> now claiming that land, his god? Ha ha! He could have laughed at the whole
> ludicrous idea, but for the fact that they had forced him into the other life, the
> life he had tried to avoid. He had been called upon to take up a temporary
> appointment as a District Officer. He had agreed. But only because this meant
> defending his god. If Mau Mau claimed the only thing he believed in, they
> would see! (pp. 76–7)

When Boro confronts him with the reasons for fighting the war,

Howlands reveals he does not comprehend that Africans have any rights whatsoever:

> 'I killed Jacobo.'
>   'I know.'
>   'He betrayed black people. Together, you killed many sons of the land. You raped our women. And finally you killed my father. Have you anything to say in your defence?'
>   Boro's voice was flat. No colour of hatred, anger or triumph. No sympathy. 'Nothing.'
>   'Nothing. Now you say nothing. But when you took our ancestral lands – '
>   'This is my land.' Mr Howlands said this as a man would say, This is my woman.
>   '*Your* land! Then, you white dog, you'll die on your land.'
>   Mr Howlands thought him mad. Fear overwhelmed him and he tried to cling to life with all his might. But before he could reach Boro, the gun went off. Boro had learnt to be a good marksman during the Second World War. The white man's trunk stood defiant for a few seconds. Then it fell down. (p. 128–9)

This is as much insight as Howland achieves.

Njoroge works in a shop owned by an Asian for a time. But such is his desolation that he does the job badly and is fired from it. At his last encounter with Mwihaki he asks her to escape from Kenya with him for Uganda – just as she had sought him to do in the past. This time it is she who refuses, and echoing Njoroge's words, speaks to him of 'duty' and 'responsibility'. There is no talk of misty dreams, but merely the need to accept the stark reality of the terror and wait it out. Mwihaki, it seems can do this, but not Njoroge.

He attempts to hang himself but is saved from doing so by his mother. The novel ends on a deeply gloomy note:

> But as they came near home and what had happened to him came to mind, the voice again came and spoke accusing him: *You are a coward. You have always been a coward. Why didn't you do it?*
>   And loudly he said, 'Why didn't I do it?'
>   The voice said: *Because you are a coward.*
>   'Yes,' he whispered to himself. 'I am a coward.'
>   And he ran home and opened the door for his two mothers. (p. 136)

Weep Not, Child is a small novel with few complexities either of plot or in the creation of characters. There is a symbolic quality in the novel. Ngugi admits having had a certain symbolism in mind when he wrote this book. He says, for example, that he saw Jomo Kenyatta as a kind of saviour or Black Messiah but admits that they are not saviours as such but:

symbols of certain social forces which are started, and the individuals are mere agents of those forces which are already in society.[5]

Similarly, Njoroge conceives an analogous symbolic role for himself, seeing the equation between Jomo and Moses and his own potential relation to it. In a way all of the characters and situations, though unmistakably real, present something more. Howlands is a typical Kenyan farmer with notions as callow and imperfectly thought through as Ngotho's unquestioning faith in Mugo's prophecy or Njoroge's callow dream of being a Messiah.

The small village of Ngotho is a microcosm of Kenya at the time of the emergency and the principal characters – Ngotho, Njoroge, Howlands, Boro, and Jacobo – represent the various points of view, possibly too obviously, which obtain in it. Certain scenes, as well, have a symbolic reference. The most notable of these is when Howlands, now partly crazed and demented with fatigue and killing, threatens to castrate Njoroge as he has done Ngotho. It is suggestive of the desire of Europeans to deprive Africans of their rights and manhood.

The creation of Njoroge is the weakest part of the book. Njoroge, we are told, 'had always been a dreamer, a visionary who consoled himself faced by the difficulties of the moment by a look at a better day to come'. This represents a weakness in the character and, by implication, in his creator. Often throughout the book he retreats into vague phrases, a measure of his inability to control, at the age he is, his destiny. Often throughout the novel he is powerless to act and does not want to contemplate the possible consequences of certain hard facts that have to be faced. Ngugi gives Njoroge more to do than a youth of his age can do and more to understand than a youth with his limited intellect can cope with.

If the viewpoint of the novel is not wholly adequate to a full examination of the theme – how much more would be gained, for example, to see the events of the novel through Boro's eyes – the disinterestedness Ngugi achieves in his rendering of the events of the book accounts for its convincingness. Njoroge's point of view is severly limited. He, like Waiyaki, never grows to intellectual maturity. His Messianic dream, not unlike Waiyaki's, of saving his people in time of trouble by means of education, vaguely defined, and the large charity found in the sacrifice of Christ, equally vaguely apprehended, is founded on adolescent romanticism. As such it is vulnerable and crumbles when pressure is applied, pressure of a kind even an adult, mature in body and will, would find difficult to withstand.

Njoroge is delicately moulded and we watch him grow from boyhood

into adolescence with an interest and compassion similar in kind to the
emotion which prompted Ngugi to create him. We know his boyish
dream is callow and we do not mind that. It is a dream that a boy can have.
Equally we feel no great pity when the dream dies. We share his fear in the
forest when the teacher is murdered by the colonial troops and sense the
horror and the pain of the castration with which the maddened Howlands
threatens him.

But this is not an idyll, not a tale for children. And so it is the events
taking place in the society in which Njoroge lives which matter most to
readers.

The dream of education, too, is another weakness in the book. The
suggestion is made that Njoroge's acquisition of western education is the
means to a better future – of acquiring the understanding of the white
man and thus of achieving what he has achieved of re-acquiring the land.
But little is made of this. Nyokabi, it seems, wants Njoroge to be educated
so that she will be able to feel the same as the Howlands women or Juliana,
the wife of Jacobo:

> That was something. That was real life. It did not matter if anyone died poor
> provided he or she could one day say, 'Look, I have a son as good and as well
> educated as any can find in the land'. (p. 16)

And while Ngotho is prepared to say that 'Education is everything' it is
the land that is everything and education useful only if it leads to the
recovery of the land. Kamau and Kori contribute to Njoroge's education
but say little about why they do so. Perhaps it is simply assumed that
readers know and nothing more needs be said.

The question of the value and the kind of education which is best for
African people is something Ngugi is much concerned with of course. It
is a central theme in *The River Between*, where the discussion is more
clearly focused than here. In this novel we see, perhaps, the beginning of
the analysis which will consume many pages in *Petals of Blood*, the
suspicion that the sort of idyllic formal education doled out in the remote
safety of such schools as Siriana merely shields people from life and that
the real lessons are learned in the informal, sometimes terrifying experiences which one is left to synthesize for himself. But the matter is left up
in the air here.

The book makes passing implicit comment on the morality of various
related actions and enterprises which form familiar themes in Ngugi's
writing. Howlands expounds the morality of paternal colonialism in
conjunction with a belief in his right to the land. So great is his obsession
with the land and his sense of betrayal on the part of Africans, that the

violence he vents on them ultimately rebounds to derange him:

> He had remembered himself as a boy, that day so long ago when he had sat
> outside his parents' home and dreamt of a world that needed him, only to be
> brought face to face with the harsh reality of life in the First World War . . . Mr
> Howlands could now remember only drinking to make himself forget. He
> cursed horribly.
>   And this Ngotho. He had let him go home more dead than alive. But still he
> had let him go. Howlands had not got the satisfaction he had hoped for. The
> only thing left to him was hatred. What had made him release Ngotho was a
> notebook that had been found behind the lavatory from where apparently
> Jacobo had been shot. The notebook had Boro's name. At first Mr Howlands
> had been unable to understand. But gradually he realized that Ngotho had been
> telling a lie, in order to shield Boro. But Boro was in the forest? Slowly he
> arrived at the truth. Ngotho too had thought that it was Kamau who had done
> the murder. He had taken on the guilt to save a son. At this Mr Howlands'
> hatred of Ngotho had been so great that he had trembled the whole night.
> (pp. 127-8)

Howlands and Boro, who eventually kills him, are not unalike in the
views they hold and practise. Ultimately simple expedience determines
and justifies how they act. Boro's thinking is somewhat confused as this
passage shows; but he honours necessity:

> 'And Freedom?' the lieutenant continued.
>   'An illusion. What Freedom is there for you and me?'
>   'Why then do we fight?'
>   'To kill. Unless you kill, you'll be killed. So you go on killing and destroying.
> It's a law of nature. The white man too fights and kills with gas, bombs, and
> everything.'
>   'But don't you think there's something wrong in fighting and killing unless
> you're doing so for a great cause like ours?'
>   'What great cause is ours?'
>   'Why, Freedom and the return of our lost heritage.'
>   'Maybe there's something in that. But for me Freedom is meaningless unless
> it can bring back a brother I lost. Because it can't do that, the only thing left to
> me is to fight, to kill and rejoice at any who falls under my sword. But enough.
> Chief Jacobo must die.' (pp. 102-3)

Boro's actions are consistent with his beliefs: when he kills Howlands he
experiences no emotion at first. He has killed out of a sense of duty.

Ngugi comments as we have seen on the morality of the preaching of
the Christian missionaries as it seeks to deflect the African from a just
consideration of his circumstances. The passage from St Matthew which
Ngugi cites offers an ironic reflection on how the missionaries, in
collusion with other European forces – a policy of Howlands in the
emergency is 'to set these people fighting amongst themselves instead of

fighting with the white men ... ' (p. 77) – have been instrumental in perpetrating the divide-and-rule policy against which the passage preaches.

Finally, this is a novel which examines various attitudes toward 'duty'. Each of the characters acts out of a sense of commitment to an idea, each believes his idea defensible and each, as the events of the novel proceed, is given cause to re-examine the strength of his position. Ngotho and Njoroge's positions change as a result of their experiences but not those of other principal characters; rather, their positions harden and they pay with their lives. Ngotho gives his life in order to save his son's, reversing the attitude which caused him to reject the oath when Boro sought to administer it to him at the emergencies' beginning – in Ngotho's mind Boro had 'no right to reverse the custom and tradition for which he and his generation stood'. In the actions and reactions of his characters, in the way he probes into motivations, in the compassion he shows for Njoroge, Ngotho, Mwihaki especially but also for Nyokabi, Nyeri and the brothers of Njoroge, Ngugi's humanism is revealed and tempers his anger.

As with *The River Between* Ngugi achieves a notable effect in a small book which in plain language and with plain and neatly balanced plotting conveys an impression of an important period in contemporary history by displaying the experiences of a variety of sensitive human beings.

Ngugi was aware of the shortcomings of the novel and its limited perspective which accounts for the uncomplicated nature of the story it tells and the motifs it examines. He accounts for this by saying that he was a child growing up during the emergency period and because of this was not aware of all the implications of the struggle. But, he says:

> One did get the impressions. You are so young. You see your uncles being killed. British soldiers come to collect your uncles. You see some of your friends being taken from their homes. These things stay with you. You see an old man you respected being emasculated as a condition of war. These things leave you with the impression though you take these things for granted and just go on.[6]

The novelist then synthesizes the personal experience into the imaginative work and is fully successful in realizing his aim which he describes in the following fashion:

> In *Weep Not, Child* I just wanted to capture as much as possible the atmosphere of the situation, what it felt like to actually live in the small village at this time. So I wasn't trying to capture anything that was very deep, but I was trying to capture what it felt like to live in a civil war. So that even if I didn't use my experience in many of the episodes, there are things which I may have seen or heard or felt at the time.[7]

There is a sparseness of concrete details of the lives of the characters, even Njoroge the most fully perceived figure in the book, and of the society in which the action takes place. So, too, there is a sparseness about the inner lives of the characters. This sparseness, accentuated by virtue of the village setting in which Ngugi places the action of the novel makes the book more a history of the changes wrought by the emergency than an experience of the change in the way a novel can convey a sense of how such changes come about.

Weep Not, Child is a small book and in some respects a naive one. But in it, as in *The River Between*, Ngugi puts down a blueprint for the mature writing in *A Grain of Wheat* and *Petals of Blood*.

REFERENCES AND NOTES

1. Jomo Kenyatta, *Facing Mount Kenya* (London: Martin Secker and Warburg 1938; Heinemann Educational Books, 1979), p.21.
2. *Ibid.*, p.
3. Ime Ikiddeh, 'Ngugi wa Thiong'o; the novelist as historian' in Bruce King and Kolawole Ogungbesan (eds.), *A Celebration of Black African Writing* (Zaria: Ahmadu Bello University Press; London: OUP 1975), p. 210.
4. Jomo Kenyatta, *op. cit.*, p. 317.
5. Reinhard Sander and Ian Munro, 'Tolstoy in Africa', *Ba Shiru*, vol. 5 (1973), p. 26.
6. *Ibid.*
7. *Ibid.*

4 *A Grain of Wheat*

▼▼▼▼▼▼▼▼▼▼▼▼▼▼▼▼▼▼▼▼▼▼▼▼▼▼▼▼▼▼▼▼▼▼

> We must repeat, it is absolutely necessary to oppose vigorously and definitely the birth of national bourgeoisie and a privileged caste. To educate the masses politically is to make the nation a reality to each citizen. It is to make the history of the nation part of the personal experience of each of its citizens.
>
> *Frantz Fanon*

A GRAIN OF WHEAT is a novel about the Mau Mau independence war. It tells the story of four principal characters (and a number of minor supporting characters) who relive, vividly, their experiences of the war in the four days leading up to the day of Kenyan independence, 12 December 1963.

The motto of the novel is found in the verses from Corinthians (I, 15:36) from which the book's title is taken:

> Thou fool, that which thou sowest is not quickened, except it die. And that which thou sowest, thou sowest not that body that shall be, but bare grain, it may chance of wheat, or of some other grain.

Given that Ngugi's interest is in character and in the moral choices that humans have to make and the reasons they advance for making them, given that he has found the technical means for conveying the psychological complexities of individual states of mind as well as the complexities of their social and personal relationships through controlled and sophisticated narrative structure, all of the principal characters can be said to reflect in their experiences in the novel, the process of birth, growth, death and rebirth implied in the Biblical quotation.

Ngugi is interested in the social circumstances of his characters and especially in the background of the Mau Mau resistance against which these figures live their lives and as they are altered by it. He makes plain what the causes of the resistance are and he is at pains, through the speeches and actions of Kihika, who symbolizes the freedom fighter, to insure that his readers know that the struggle was a just one. But the background is kept firmly in control. Ngugi wants principally to examine the fragility of human life as this is revealed through an understanding of the secret lives of his characters – their states of mind as these are the product of the violence of the independence struggle.

The four principal characters are Mugo, Gikonyo, Mumbi and Karanja and these four days of their lives are dominated by their remembrance of Kihika, a famous freedom fighter, the brother of Mumbi, for all but one of them a boyhood friend. Kihika was betrayed to the British by one of the villagers and was hanged. His comrades in arms, General R. and Lt Koinandu who have survived the struggle come to the village, Thabai, to discover the betrayer and denounce him at the Uhura celebrations.

Uhura Day, the day when independence from the colonial power is achieved, has been the dream of each of these figures from their school-days. But there is little joyousness in their lives as they recall over the four days their experiences of the war and its aftermath. Ngugi is able to make time present and time past coincident by the narrative technique he adopts. Thus he strips away the layers of their lives and each character, at the novel's close, stands fully revealed. As well, out of the recollections of these people we come to know Kihika and understand the motives which made him a forest fighter.

Ngugi elaborates and deepens the materials of *Weep Not, Child*. *A Grain of Wheat* is the work of a writer more mature than when he wrote his first two books. In the first books he told us what his people felt, and their hopes and fears were conveyed in language which was often generalized and sometimes vague. In *A Grain of Wheat* he takes us into the minds of his characters, sensibilities resonant with ambiguities and contradictions, and causes us to feel what they feel, to share in significant measure their hopes and fears and pain. Not their joy, however. There is little joy in the novel and what there is produces ironic results.

Ngugi has developed a complex narrative structure in which he moves quickly and easily back and forth between various periods in time. He does this because he is primarily interested in the inner lives, in the mental states of his characters and his aim in attempting to account for the present mental states of his characters is to show how these are the product of events, layer upon layer, moving forward from past time. The aim is, really, to make time present and time past coincident. Thus, he employs a number of devices to create a chronology which is lacking in linear form. The novel is a montage made up of narrative passages, interior monologues, dialogue, recollections and anecdotes. *Lord Jim* is often cited by critics who discuss Ngugi's book and it would seem plain that Ngugi has learned much about his craft from Conrad.[1] Conrad placed his characters in situations designed to test their moral strength. When they are found wanting – as they always are – he examines why this is so by displaying their guilt-ridden recollections, reflections – the inner workings of their minds. Because of his sympathy for his characters and because he enjoins our own sympathy, Ngugi reveals the sources of guilt gradually over the course of the novel. So by the novel's close, the characters stand fully exposed to themselves and to us. We are intimate with the principal characters. We have their views of themselves and we know what they think of each other.

The novel is about the Mau Mau war and we learn more about it than we did in *Weep Not, Child* precisely because Ngugi knows more about, understands better the causes and prosecution of the independence struggle and is able to convey his understanding in a book of a size which matches his understanding. So while we find in *A Grain of Wheat* the same materials as in *Weep Not, Child* we see them from a greater variety of and from more complicated perspectives. As with *Weep Not, Child* in *A Grain of Wheat* we are made to understand the consequences, both physical and psychological, of the emergency. Not only are the points of view offered more plentiful but they are represented by adults who are capable not only of feeling deeply (Njoroge could do that) but of giving expression to their feelings and of scrutinizing them.

One of the fundamental themes of the novel is betrayal and the consequent need of the betrayer to expiate the sense of guilt that results. The novel conveys through the complexity of its tiered time framework when we exist in a series of coincident 'presents', the mental suffering that recollections and the quest for forgiveness occasion. The independence struggle is important to Ngugi and he has written this novel to explain, in artistic terms, and through a sustained comparison with Christian teaching, action and theology, the origins of the struggle and especially its legitimacy. He does this in detail, drawing in much of the same historical and political material as he has used in *Weep Not, Child* and *The River Between*. Thus we learn again of the creation of Mumbi and Gikuyu to whom the land – the source of life – is given. We hear of the prophecy of Mugo wa Kibiro, of the 'butterflies', the white men, who would come with their God and their guns to dispossess the people of the land. A pattern, familiar in history of human kind, reproduces itself in Kenya:

About Jesus, they could not at first understand, for how could it be God would let himself be nailed to a tree? The whiteman spoke of that Love that passeth all

understanding. Greater Love hath no man than this, he read from the little
black book, that a man lay down his life for his friends.

The few who were converted, started speaking a faith foreign to the ways of
the land. They trod on sacred places to show that no harm could reach those
protected by the hand of the Lord. Soon people saw the whiteman had
imperceptibly acquired more land to meet the growing needs of his position.
He had already pulled down the grass-thatched hut and erected a more
permanent building. Elders of the land protested. They looked beyond the
laughing face of the whiteman and suddenly saw a long line of other red
strangers who carried, not the Bible, but the sword. (p. 12)

Ngugi lists the names of those Kenyans who martyred themselves, over
a fifty-year period, for Kenya's independence. The list includes Waiyaki,
Harry Thuku, and Jomo Kenyatta and their activities are briefly sketched
in to show their inspirational effect on Kihika. Kihika sees in Waiyaki's
failure and death, the seeds of future successes:

Waiyaki and other warrior-leaders took arms. The iron snake spoken of by
Mugo wa Kibiro was quickly wriggling towards Nairobi for a thorough
exploitation of the hinterland. Could they move it? The snake held on to the
ground, laughing their efforts to scorn. The whiteman with bamboo poles that
vomited fire and smoke, hit back; his menacing laughter remained echoing in
the hearts of the people, long after Waiyaki had been arrested and taken to the
coast, bound hands and feet. Later, so it is said, Waiyaki was buried alive at
Kibwezi with head facing into the centre of the earth, a living warning to those,
who, in after years, might challenge the hand of the Christian woman whose
protecting shadow now bestrode both land and sea.

Then nobody noticed it; but looking back we can see that Waiyaki's blood
contained within it a seed, a grain, which gave birth to a political party whose
main strength thereafter sprang from a bond with the soil. (p. 13)

The novel depicts and dramatizes the emergency in more detail and on
a broader canvas than *Weep Not, Child* even though the subject-matter is
the same. We have the view of the whole nation being involved as this is
suggested through a much larger community offered as representative of
the experience of Kenyans. Moreover, there is a larger community of
whites, British for the most part, and we see the forces of the belief in the
'civilizing mission' with its emphasis on a benevolent paternalism. This
theme is consolidated in John Thompson. Thompson's vision of the
British Empire as a 'great moral idea' is jotted down in his notes for a book
he is writing. *Prospero in Africa* reveals a national habit of mind just as
Thompson's own experiences of Oxford, a love of Kipling, an understanding of Lugard's achievement in Africa prompts his vision:

Transform the British Empire into one nation: didn't this explain so many
things, why, for instance, so many Africans had offered themselves up to die in
the war against Hitler?

From the first, as soon as he set his hands on a pen to write down his thoughts, the title of the manuscript floated before him. He would call it: PROSPERO IN AFRICA. In it he argued that to be English was basically an attitude of mind: it was a way of looking at life, at human relationship, at the just ordering of human society. Was it not possible to reorientate people into this way of life by altering their social and cultural environment? *Prospero in Africa* was a result of an assiduous dive into English history, and the General History of Colonization from the Roman times to the present day. He was influenced by the French policy of Assimilation but was critical of the French as he was of what he called 'Lugard's retrograde concept of Indirect Rule!' 'We must avoid the French mistake of assimilating only the educated few. The peasant in Asia and Africa must be included in this moral scheme of rehabilitation. In Great Britain we have had our peasant, and now our worker, and they are no less an integral part of our society'. (p. 48)

Thompson, the most prominent of the European characters in the novel, is used by Ngugi to show the British reaction to the independence struggle. As with the Europeans in the other novels Ngugi deals with the character objectively. He understands, even though he cannot condone them, Thompson's motives. If the way these motives are displayed in Thompson's notebooks and ruminations appear naive it is because they were naive, the whole basis of the dream of civilizing Africa as Thompson enunciates it is naive. The pattern is Thompson's disintegration, mentally and spiritually, rendered in a series of entries in his diary. Ngugi shows how Thompson, an ordinary, decent man, changes when the ideal he serves is challenged:

Nyeri is full of mountains, hills and deep valleys covered with impenetrable forests. These primordial trees have always awed primitive minds. The darkness and mystery of the forest, have led him (the primitive man) to magic and ritual.

What's this thing called Mau Mau?

Dr Albert Schweitzer says 'The Negro is a child, and with children, nothing can be done without the use of authority.' I've now worked in Nyeri, Githima, Kisumu, Ngong. I agree.

I am back in Nyeri. People are moving into villages to cut the connection between them and the terrorists. Burning houses in the old village, suddenly I felt my life was coming to a cul de sac.

Colonel Robson, a Senior District Officer in Rung'ei, Kiambu, was savagely murdered. I am replacing him at Rung'ei. One must use a stick. No government can tolerate anarchy, no civilization can be built on this violence and savagery. Mau Mau is evil: a movement which if not checked will mean complete destruction of all the values on which our civilization has thriven.

Every whiteman is continually in danger of gradual moral ruin in this daily and hourly contest with the African. Dr Albert Schweitzer.

In dealing with the African you are often compelled to do the unexpected. A man came into my office yesterday. He told me about a wanted terrorist leader. From the beginning, I was convinced the man was lying, was really acting, perhaps to trap me or hide his own part in the movement. He seemed to be laughing at me. Remember the African is a born actor, that's why he finds it so easy to lie. Suddenly I spat into his face. I don't know why, but I did it. (pp. 49–50)

Eventually a man with a promising career in front of him – 'D.C., P.C. – A Governor' makes himself into a monster inflicting savage punishment on the inmates at Ria camp where he sanctions the deaths of eleven prisoners.

In the end it proves to be that there is no moral base to Thompson's position. When he discovers this he lashes out, blaming others for his own want of understanding. He seeks scapegoats and finds them.

There is no lack of certitude in Kihika. There is a certain pomposity about him and a tendency to show off, to draw attention to himself through the chances he takes, first at school and later in his deeds of daring in the Mau Mau struggle, culminating in his shooting of D. O. Robson, an act which wins him immortality as well as death. General R. tells us that Kihika talked too much while others went out and fought. These touches of characterization humanize Kihika, a figure who, because he embodies for Ngugi both the values and the spirit of the independence fighter, might easily have become a caricature.

Kihika is the only one of the principal characters who is not alive in the present time setting of the novel. Yet his spirit dominates the events of the Uhuru Day celebrations and the thoughts of the other main figures, Mumbi, Mugo and Gikonyo.

Kihika has the Messianic vision of Waiyaki and Njoroge, the experience, courage and resourcefulness of Boro and an articulateness which exceeds each of them:

'It's a question of Unity,' Kihika explained excitedly. 'The example of India is there before our noses. The British were there for hundreds and hundreds of years. They ate India's wealth. They drank India's blood. They never listened to the political talk-talk of a few men. What happened? There came this man Gandhi. Mark you, Gandhi knows his whiteman well. He goes round and organizes the Indian masses into a weapon stronger than the bomb. They say with one voice: we want back our freedom. The British laughed; they are good at laughing. But they had to swallow back their laughter when things turned out serious. What did the tyrants do? They sent Gandhi to prison, not once, but many times. The stone-walls of prison could not hold him. Thousands were

gaoled; thousands more were killed. Men and women and children threw
themselves in front of moving trains and were run over. Blood flowed like water
in that country. The bomb could not kill blood, red blood of people, crying to
be free. God! How many times must fatherless children howl, widowed women
cry on this earth before this tyrant shall learn?' (p. 77)

It is Kihika who in dying, fulfils the adolescent destiny he conceives for
himself. Brought up in the Christian tradition, the correspondence
between the Gikuyu and Christian creation myths apparent to him,
Kihika sees early on that the doctrine was used to seduce the people from
the land. The Bible becomes a model for the course of action he will
follow. Adept in argument and shrewd in political judgement (aware as
well of the historical paradox which reveals time and again that faith in
the Christian God does not hold sway over political antagonisms,
however rational they might seem to be), Kihika turns the language of the
Christians on themselves. There is no paradox in his assertion:

'Yes – I said [Jesus] he had failed because his death did not change anything, it
did not make his people find a centre in the cross. All oppressed people have a
cross to bear. The Jews refused to carry it and were scattered like dust all over
the earth. Had Christ's death a meaning for the children of Israel? In Kenya we
want a death which will change things, that is to say, we want a true sacrifice.
But first we have to be ready to carry the cross. I die for you, you die for me, we
become a sacrifice for one another. So I can say that you, Karanja, are Christ. I
am Christ. Everybody who takes the Oath of Unity to change things in Kenya is
a Christ.' (p. 83)

The passages which are underlined in Kihika's Bible and which Ngugi
uses as mottos in the book – from Revelations 21:1, I Corinthians 15:36
and St John 12:24 – all serve to give legitimacy, authenticity and support
to Kihika's mission. It is from the passage in Corinthians that the title of
the novel is derived. For Ngugi the passages from the Bible have an
association with the situation in Kenya in which sacrifice is called for and
in which assurance of the legitimacy of the sacrifices made is needed. St
Paul answers the Corinthians who have misgivings about the resurrection
of the mortal body and about the Second Coming:

Thou fool, that which thou sowest is not quickened, except it die. And that
which thou sowest, thou sowest not that body that shall be, but bare grain, it
may chance of wheat, or of some other grain.[2]

This passage taken together with the others form a continuum which
asserts that sacrifice will prompt change and draw attention to the reasons
for the sacrifice. This in turn will draw attention to the possibility of
achieving the new Jerusalem according to the vision of St John, the
Divine. The paradox of the death that prompts new life to the Second

Coming and to the possibility of a new heaven and a new earth is associated in the novel with Mugo wa Kibiro, Waiyaki and Harry Thuku. Kihika is the most recent addition to the list of legendary names. And in their way each of the characters left alive after the struggles achieves a new birth on Uhuru Day.

The novel reveals an intimacy with Biblical teaching which Ngugi uses as a metaphoric framework for the story he tells. The basic analogy is with the plight of the Israelites in Egypt and it comes as no surprise to learn that the following passage is underlined in Kihika's Bible:

And the Lord said, I have surely seen the affliction of my people which are in Egypt, and have heard their cry by reason of their taskmasters; for I know their sorrows.[3]

Ngugi shows us the afflication of the people. His point of view is that of the victims of the emergency. We have reports of Kihika's activities – especially of the incident which earned him a place among the martyrs of the land, the killing of D.O. Robson. But this is reported by Kihika to Mugo. What it was like to be with the forest fighters is always reported. We never travel into the bush to be with them.

But we know the extent of their successes, by the extent of suffering of those left behind us, and it is their experiences during the prolonged emergency which establish the pattern of betrayals with which the book is fundamentally concerned of the four main figures. Three – Gikonyo, Mumbi and Karanja – are from the same village. Mugo is an outsider. He has not shared in the youthful experience with Kihika that they have. While they have a sense of common purpose they find they are not only unable to join Kihika in the forests but also unable to sustain their individual integrity.

Mugo is by far the most complex and because he is the catalyst to the resolutions of the problems of all the other characters, Ngugi is most exact in rendering him. The almost catatonic despair Mugo experiences when the novel opens has its origins in his childhood. An orphan, brought up by a drunken aunt in an atmosphere of poverty, filth and the perpetual stench of vomit, Mugo acquires from his youth a taste for isolation. Nevertheless, he determines to put the squalor of his life behind him and force society to recognize his success. Mugo is motivated by practical matters and his antagonism to Kihika, complex as this is, has its beginnings in the fact that Mugo's life is governed by practical concerns. Thus he is both offended and challenged by Kihika's idealism. When Kihika talks of 'the great sacrifice' to come, of a day 'when brother shall give up brother, a mother her son, when you and I have heard the call of a nation in turmoil':

> Mugo felt a constriction in his throat. He could not clap for words that did not touch him. What right had such a boy, probably younger than Mugo, to talk like that? What arrogance? Kihika had spoken of blood as easily as if he was talking of drawing water in a river, Mugo reflected a revulsion starting in his stomach at the sight and smell of blood. I hate him, he heard himself say and frightened, he looked at Mumbi, wondering what she was thinking. Her eyes were still fixed on her brother. Everybody's eyes were on the platform. Mugo experienced a twang of jealousy as he too turned and looked at the speaker. At that moment their eyes met, or so Mugo imagined, with guilt. For a split second the crowd and the world at large seemed drenched in silence. Only Kihika and Mugo were left on the stage. Something surged for release in Mugo's heart, something, in fact, which was an intense vibration of terror and hatred.(p. 15)

Ngugi evokes complex responses in us toward Mugo. His betrayal of Kihika is induced partly by his jealousy, partly because the disruption in the land threatens his determination never again to experience the destitution of his childhood, and partly because he simply wants not to be drawn into connections with other people. All of this is summed up in his confessional speech at the novel's close:

> 'I wanted to live my life. I never wanted to be involved in anything. Then he came into my life, here, a night like this, and pulled me into the stream. So I killed him.' (p. 161)

The confession is not entirely adequate or true, as the motives of jealousy which prompt him to go to Thompson have shown. But he is right in saying that he is drawn into 'the stream' not because of his touch with Kihika, but because of reasons that have nothing to do with the struggle. The scene is in Thabai after Mugo has betrayed Kihika to Thompson:

> He worked a few yards from the woman. He had worked in the same place for three days. Now a homeguard jumped into the trench and lashed the woman with a whip. Mugo felt the whip eat into his flesh, and her pained whimper was like a cry from his own heart. Yet he did not know her, had for three days refused to recognize those around him as fellow sufferers. Now he only saw the woman, the whip, and the homeguard. Most people continued digging, pretending not to hear the woman's screams, and fearing to meet a similar fate. Others furtively glanced at the woman as they raised their shovels and jembes. In terror, Mugo pushed forward and held the whip before the homeguard could hit the woman a fifth time. More homeguards and two or three soldiers ran to the scene. Other people temporarily stopped digging and watched the struggle and the whips that now descended on Mugo's body. 'He's mad,' some people later said, after Mugo had been taken away in a police van. To Mugo the scene remained a nightmare whose broken and blurred edges he could not pick or reconstruct during the secret screening that later followed. (p. 150)

Mugo's betrayal of Kihika is in some part mitigated by the suffering he experiences in the various detention camps he is put in because of his defence of Wambuku. But our sympathy for him really proceeds from Ngugi's skill in taking us into a mind that is collapsing under the burden of guilt it bears:

> When at long last Mugo extricated himself from Warui, he found the incident had disturbed him in a way he could not explain. He wandered through the streets thinking about the old woman and that thrilling bond he felt existed between them. Then he tried to dismiss the incident. But as he went on, he found himself starting at the thought of meeting a dead apparition. Life itself seemed a meaningless wandering. There was surely no connection between sunrise and sunset, between today and tomorrow. Why then was he troubled by what was dead, he thought, remembering the old woman. And immediately he heard Mumbi's voice in his heart and saw General R.'s face looking at him. He stood at an open space in the village. His lower lip dropped: he felt energy leave him. Weak in body, he leaned against a small tree and gradually slipped down on to the grass. He held his head in both hands. It is not me, he whispered to convince himself. It is not me, it would have happened . . . the murder of women and men in the trench . . . even if . . . even if . . . He was moaning. Mumbi's voice was a knife which had butchered and laid naked his heart to himself. The road from his hut led to the trench. But would it not have happened? Christ would have died on the cross, anyway. Why did they blame Judas, a stone from the hands of a power more than man? Kihika . . . crucified . . . the thought flashed through him, and a curious thing happened. Mugo saw thick blood dripping from the mud walls of his hut. Why had he not seen it earlier, he now wondered, almost calmly, without fear. But he was shaking as he walked out to his hut, resolved to find out if the blood was really there.
>
> He saw nothing on the wall. He sat on his bed and again propped his head in both hands. Was he cracking in the head? He started at the thought and again looked at the walls. (p. 152)

This is Mugo's nadir. After this he moves under Mumbi's benign (if unsuspecting) influence to confess his betrayal. Karanja is the agent of his confession. Mugo will not let Karanja bear the blame for Kihika's death. He will not sacrifice another person. Any temptation to do so passes quickly. His need to cleanse his soul is too strong to be denied. He makes his confession before the assembled villagers on Uhuru Day:

> As soon as the first words were out, Mugo felt light. A load of many years was lifted from his shoulders. He was free . . .

But for a moment it seems, his act has rebounded on him:

> No sooner had he finished speaking than the silence around, the lightness within, and the sudden freedom pressed heavy on him. His vision became blurred at the edges. Panic seized him, as he descended the platform, moved through the people, who were now silent. He was conscious of himself, of every

step he made, of the images that rushed and whirled through his mind with only one constant thread: so he was responsible for whatever he had done in the past, for whatever he would do in the future. The consciousness frightened him. Nothing would now, this minute, make him return to that place. Suppose all those people had risen and dug their nails and teeth into his body? (p. 204)

Mugo seeks shelter from the first drops of rain in the hut of the village mad woman, the mother of the mute Gitogo who was the first victim from the village in the emergency. And here, in a moment of visionary acuteness, Mugo makes the tragic and pathetic recognition that one cannot escape one's destiny:

> She walked towards him. But Mugo was not listening to her wild muttering. For suddenly her face had changed. Mugo looked straight into the eyes of his aunt. A new rage moved him. Life was only a constant repetition of what happened yesterday and the day before. Only this time she would not escape. He would stop that oblique smile, that contemptuous glint in the eyes. But before he could move, the woman staggered back into her seat. The smile still lingered on her face. She did not move or make the slightest stir. And suddenly he knew: the only person who had ever claimed him was dead. He buried his face in his hands and stood thus for a few seconds. (p. 205)

Ngugi exploits moments such as these – what Joyce calls an 'epiphany' – in his novels. We recall the moment in *The River Between* when Waiyaki has 'a momentary vision that flashed across his mind and seemed to light the dark corners of his soul'.[4] Mugo's glimpse of ultimate truth clears his mind of the demons that have possessed it:

> There was nothing on the walls: no visions of blood, no galloping footsteps behind him, no detention camps, and Mumbi seemed a vague thing in a remote past. Occasionally he tapped the bed frame, almost irritably. (p. 205)

The drop of water, grown fat and dirty which threatens to engulf him in the tortured dream with which the story opens is translated into a cleansing rain, symbolizing his regeneration, a baptism for a new life, as it were:

> Water dripped from his hair, down to his face and neck in broken lines; water dripped from his coat, again in broken lines, down his legs and on to the ground. A drop was caught in his right eyelashes and the light from the lamp was split into many tiny lashes. Then the drop entered his eye, melted inside, and ran down his face like a tear. (pp. 205–6)

After a scene such as this, General R.'s monomaniacal quest for vengeance seems spurious and Ngugi with fine artistic judgement, brings the scene quickly to a close. General R. has no inkling of the fine irony which informs his last words to Mugo:

> 'Your deeds alone will condemn you,' General R. continued without anger or

apparent bitterness. 'You – No one will ever escape from his own actions.'
(p. 206)

Mugo is associated with the passage from St John. His death in the
present, ironically when his heroism was to be made plain to all, is
compared to Kihika's death in the past. Kihika sacrifices himself so that a
new heaven and new earth might be achieved. Mugo, whose sacrifice is on
a less elevated level, sacrifices himself so that others' sins may be absolved.
Mugo's existence will gain significance only in death.

Mumbi has been the unwitting agent of Mugo's regeneration, just as
he becomes for her, and for her husband Gikonyo. For Mumbi's guilty
secret, the explanation for the bitterness Gikonyo has for her has become
unbearable to her, just as Mugo's has for him. And like his, her guilt has
its origins in the emergency period. The love between Mumbi and
Gikonyo began in their adolescence. Timid of declaring his love for her
and fearful she will reject him, Gikonyo, for a long time, keeps his feelings
to himself. But Mumbi shows Gikonyo she favours him over other suitors
and in one of the few scenes of lyrical happiness in the novel Ngugi shows
us the rapture of their recognition of their love. But Gikonyo becomes
involved in the insurrection.

Gikonyo goes to prison with a firm faith in the useful outcome of the
emergency:

> Gikonyo walked towards detention with a brisk step and an assurance born in
> his knowledge of love and life. This thing would end soon, anyway. Jomo would
> win the case, his lawyers having come all the way from the land of the whiteman
> and from Gandhi's India. The day of deliverance was near at hand. Gikonyo
> would come back and take the thread of life, but this time in a land of glory and
> plenty. This is what he wanted to tell his mother and Mumbi as the soldiers led
> him to the waiting truck. Let the whiteman then do anything; the day would
> come, indeed was near at hand when he would rejoin Thabai and, together with
> those who had taken to the forest, would rock the earth with a new song at the
> birth of freedom. (pp. 90–1)

But his resolve is sorely tested and weakened by the news that Jomo has
lost his case, has been tried and found guilty. It is weakened further when
Gatu, the abiding good spirit among the prisoners at Yala camp, hangs
himself out of despair. He experiences, eventually, a period of madness
induced by the psychological terror of life in the camps:

> He struggled to recall the outline of Mumbi's face without success; there was
> only a succession of images each one cancelling out the one immediately
> preceding it. Was he dead? He put his hand on his chest, felt the heart-beat and
> knew that he was alive. Why then couldn't he fix a permanent outline of Mumbi
> in his mind? Perhaps she too had dissolved into the mist. He tried to relive the
> scene in the wood and was surprised to see he could not experience anything;

the desire, the full manhood, the haunting voice of Mumbi, the explosion, no feeling came even as a thing of the past. And all this time, Gikonyo watched himself act – his every gesture his flow of thought. He was both in and outside of himself – in a trance, considering everything calmly, and only mildly puzzled by the failure of his memory. Maybe I'm weary, the thought crossed his mind. If I stand up, everything that makes me what I am will rush back into activity. So he stood up and indeed things seemed to rush back into activity. The room, for instance went round and round – he attempted to walk; panic suddenly seized him, he staggered against the wall, a grunt emitted from his mouth as he slumped back on to the floor, into total darkness. (pp. 97–8)

When he achieves his health he renounces the oath and returns to Mumbi, destined to live with the treachery his renunciation implies and seeing it as futile. Mumbi, for love of whom he took the action, now nurses Karanja's child. This accounts for his rejection of Mumbi.

There are many correspondences between Gikonyo and Mugo. Each is, in a sense, an orphan: Mugo's parents are dead and Gikonyo's have driven him from their house. Each seeks to achieve independence and security and are prepared to work for it – Mugo as a farmer and Gikonyo as a carpenter. In a real sense their work is their life. Gikonyo's affection for the wood he works with is of a kind with Mugo's for the soil he cultivates:

Holding a plane, smoothing a piece of wood, all this sent a thrill of fear and wonder through the young man. The smell of wood fascinated him. Soon his senses developed sharp discrimination, so that he could tell any type of wood by a mere sniff. (p. 64)

The psychological well-being of both Mugo and Gikonyo is determined by their responses to these materials of their livelihood. For Mugo, after the emergency, bearing his guilty secret, the soil becomes a metaphor for his soul: 'dry and hollow, tumble down' (p. 7).

Gikonyo, who cannot bear the depredation of prison, forswears his oath and returns to find his wife has betrayed him, abandons his craft as carpenter to become a successful petty trader. But the activity produces none of the satisfaction that his work with wood produced in the past. At the end of the novel when his soul has been purged of the black jealousy which has so long possessed him, he takes up again the idea of carving a stool for Mumbi as a wedding gift. He had conceived the idea of carving the stool when years before he heard her express affection for traditional stools. In detention he takes his mind off his sordid state by considering motifs for the stool he will eventually carve. But he abandons the idea during the long period after his return to Thabai when relations between Mumbi and himself are antagonistic.

Gikonyo is a straightforward person who deals in plain talk and is incapable of duplicity. Thus, when he finds that Mumbi has borne a child by Karanja he conceives his visions of her treachery that, in the psychological agony they provoke, exact a punishment on himself for his betrayal of himself. His confession to Mugo – the state of mind that it reveals and the motives that provoke it – are better understood by Mugo than Gikonyo could suspect. Ngugi secures the unity of the novel by discovering and exploiting numbers of parallel circumstances such as this one:

'Anyway, I must have gone mad. I suppose there is nothing so painful as finding that a friend, or a man you always trusted, has betrayed you. Anyway, when later I woke up, I found myself in bed and a blanket covered me. The oil-lamp, just like this one here, was burning feebly, like something diseased, know what I mean? Even the smell of everything reminded you of a scene in hospital. My mother sat beside the bed. Mumbi stood a few feet away. I could not see her face clearly, but I thought she had been crying. For a moment, a minute, you might say, something rippled in my heart. Mumbi, the woman I knew, could not let Karanja into her bed. She was the same as I had left her. Then I saw the child. And I knew that what I had thought impossible had happened. My teeth started clattering and I shuddered all over, as if I had caught a cold and a fever, malaria. Yet now I had lost all desire to kill her. It was then that I made a decision: I would never talk about the child. I would continue life as if nothing had happened. But I would never enter Mumbi's bed. What more was there for me to do but to give myself wholly to work, hard work?' Gikonyo searched Mugo's face. He could not discern anything. The silence made him uncomfortable. It seemed as if the whole thing was a repetition of a familiar scene. (p. 106)

Just as Mugo re-enacts his life in the four days leading up to Uhuru, a re-enactment that culminates in the momentary gleam of profound insight, so the same pattern produces itself in Gikonyo's mind and life. At the celebration he enters a foot race and his main opponent is Karanja, father of Mumbi's bastard child, Gikonyo's ancient rival for her love. The race is a re-enactment of the race to the railway platform years before, which Gikonyo lost to Karanja but which, paradoxically, won him Mumbi. The same thing happens again, and the race becomes a contest not between himself and Karanja, but between them for Mumbi. Gikonyo stumbles, is injured and taken to hospital. There he hears of Mugo's confession which becomes the agent for his personal catharsis:

For the last three days he thought of Mugo and the confession. Could he, Gikonyo, gather such courage to tell people about the steps on the pavement? At night he went over his life and his experiences in the seven detention camps. What precisely had all these years brought him? At every thought, he was pricked with guilt. Courage had failed him, he had confessed the oath in spite of vows to the contrary. What difference was there between him and Karanja or

Mugo or those who had openly betrayed people and worked with the whiteman to save themselves? Mugo had the courage to face his guilt and lose everything. Gikonyo shuddered at the thought of losing everything. But after Mugo's confession, he found himself trying to puzzle out Mumbi's thoughts and feelings. What lay hidden behind her face? What did she think of Mugo and the confession? He increasingly longed to speak to her about Mugo and then about his own life in detention. (pp. 211–12)

Mumbi is the least complicated of the four main characters in the novel and Gikonyo, whose sense of betrayal by her proceeds from a personal morality so pure that it can tolerate nothing less than total fidelity, is too hard on her. Her quest in life is a simple one:

'Even when I got married, the dream did not die. I longed to make my husband happy, yes, but I also prepared myself to stand by him when the time came. I could carry his sheath and as fast as he shot into the enemy, I would feed him with arrows. If danger came and he fell, he would fall into my arms and I would bring him home safely to myself.'
He saw the light at the bottom of the pool dancing in her eyes. He felt her dark power over him.
'Yet when they took him away, I did nothing, and when he finally came home, tired, I could no longer make him happy.' (p. 120)

As Mumbi makes plain in her account to Mugo, in giving herself to Karanja at the time when he brings her the news of Gikonyo's release from prison, the sexual encounter became the ultimate extension of her supreme joy in hearing of her husband's release and Karanja becomes merely an agent in the process.

'What else is there to tell you? That I remember being full of submissive gratitude? That I laughed – even welcomed Karanja's cold lips on my face? I was in a strange world, and it was like if I was mad. And need I tell you more? I let Karanja make love to me.' (pp. 131-2)

Gikonyo's frenzied imaginings of an adulterous affair between Mumbi and Karanja account for his disaffection for her and corrode his mind. He never asks, and therefore can never know Mumbi's feelings when the height of the emotion has passed:

'When I woke and realized fully what had happened, I became cold, the whole body. Karanja tried to say nice things to me, but I could see he was laughing at me with triumph. I took one of his shoes and I threw it at him. I ran out, and I could not cry. Although a few minutes before, I had been so happy, now I only felt sour inside. I went to Wangari and this time I cried and I could not clearly tell her what had happened. But she seemed to understand, and she held me to her and tried to remove my shivers with words.' (p. 132)

Mumbi is made to suffer too much by Gikonyo and almost too late he realizes the price she has paid for her steadfastness toward him. He seeks to re-establish their life together but learns that this will be done on her terms:

> 'No, Gikonyo. People try to rub out things, but they cannot. Things are not so easy. What has passed between us is too much to be passed over in a sentence. We need to talk, to open our hearts to one another, examine them, and then together plan the future we want. But now, I must go, for the child is ill.' (p. 213)

These are the terms he is prepared to accept:

> 'Will you – will you come tomorrow?' he asked, unable to hide his anxiety and fear. He knew, at once, that in future he would reckon with her feelings, her thoughts, her desires – a new Mumbi. (p. 213)

Gikonyo, in his decision to carve the stool for Mumbi, indicates that he can forgive and forget the past and that his love for Mumbi has returned. She knows now that he will accept the child. Perhaps she will accept the stool – a wedding stool – the symbol of a new beginning and a new birth.

Of the four main characters in the novel Karanja is the most pathetic and – the one who comes closest to being used purely symbolically by Ngugi. The other characters represent the various ways in which ordinary people with ordinary aspirations become victims of forces beyond themselves and what the consequences of the involvement and actions are. This is true of Karanja, of course, to a considerable extent but he is not an innocent in the way the others are. He represents the mentality of the colonized African as exactly as Kihika represents the opposite. Convinced of the superiority of the white man, he becomes his toady, first as a home guard and chief during the emergency – the repugnance Ngugi feels for this sort of betrayal of a people by one of their own is epitomized in Karanja's attitude toward Mumbi after he has seduced her.

Later, Karanja works at the research station and exploits his obsequious behaviour toward the white personnel to enhance his standing among his fellow Africans.

Ngugi humanizes Karanja and accounts for his behaviour by showing us Karanja's conviction that the world is callous and indifferent. The scene which specifies this is the weekly gathering on Sunday at the railway station. Karanja is with the others of the village who await the arrival of the train. He has raced with Gikonyo and he has won. But Mumbi has lingered behind with Gikonyo. Karanja feels desolate. The train's arrival affords Karanja a moment of utter clarity of perception that Ngugi gives each of the main characters in the novel.

Suddenly the whistle shrilled, the train pulled out of the station, and Karanja, who was watching it intently, had a strange experience. First the whistle had shrilled and the coaches clinked into his flesh. (This sensation in fact tickled through him long after the train had gone.) Then he was standing on the edge of the platform and staring into a white blank abyss. He saw this clearly, he could swear afterwards. The rails, the people at the platform, the Rung'ei shops, the whole country went in circles, faster and faster, before his eyes and then abruptly stopped. People stopped talking. Nothing moved or made a noise. Karanja was frightened by this absolute cessation of all motion and noise and he looked about him to confirm the truth of what he saw. But nothing had stopped. Everybody was running away as if each person feared the ground beneath his feet would collapse. They ran in every direction; men trampled on women; mothers forgot their children; the lame and the weak were abandoned on the platform. Each man was alone, with God. It was the clarity of the entire vision that shook him. Karanja braced himself for the struggle, the fight to live. I must clear out of this place, he told himself, without moving. The earth was going round again. I must run, he thought, it cannot be helped, why should I fear to trample on the children, the lame and the weak when others are doing it? (p. 82)

Consistent with this perception he allies himself with what he perceives to be the greatest strength, the Europeans. As well, Karanja, like Gikonyo, knows he is not made of the stuff of heroes. He is not prepared to go even as far as Gikonyo in service to the cause. His youthful contempt for Kihika - like that felt by Mugo - together with his sense of self-preservation and his hope of winning the love of Mumbi forestalls any thoughts he might have had of joining the cause:

He had gone to see Kihika hang from a tree. He had searched his heart for one has pity or sorrow for a lost friend. Instead, he found only disgust; the body was hideous; the dry lips over which a few flies played, were ugly. What is freedom? Karanja had asked himself. Was death like that Freedom? Was going to detention freedom? Was any separation from Mumbi freedom? Soon after this, he confessed the oath and joined the homeguards to save his own life. His first job was in a hood. The hood - a white sack - covered all his body except the eyes. During the screening operations, people would pass in queues in front of the hooded man. By a nod of the head, the hooded man picked out those involved in Mau Mau. (p. 199)

The image of the hood hovers before Karanja as he leaves Thabai at the close of the Uhuru Day celebrations. The accuser, symbolically, becomes the accused.

Worse than his activities as informer were his activities in the home guard, activities he recalls in his final scene of the novel:

But why am I afraid of dying, he asked himself, remembering the many men, terrorists, he and other homeguards led by their white officers, had shot dead? Then, somehow, he had not felt guilty. When he shot them, they seemed less

like human beings and more like animals. At first this had merely thrilled
Karanja and made him feel a new man, a part of an invisible might whose
symbol was the whiteman. Later, this consciousness of power, this ability to
dispose of human life by merely pulling a trigger, so obsessed him that it
became a need. Now, that power had gone. (p. 199)

For Mugo, Mumbi and Gikonyo Uhuru Day has produced freedom,
freedom of an unexpected kind – from guilt and doubt and fear. But no
such freedom will come to Karanja. He escapes the punishment that
General R. prepares for him, only to leave with the remembrance of the
evil deeds he has done, forever 'conscious ... of many angry eyes
watching him in the dark' (p. 200).

The Uhuru celebrations, which from the outset were pervaded by 'a
disturbing sense of an inevitable doom', are a failure when viewed in
terms of the villagers' expectations of what they would hear from Mugo
about the deeds he did to make Uhuru possible. Ironically, he becomes
the agent dispelling the guilt of Mumbi and, especially, Gikonyo:

'He was a brave man, inside,' he said. 'He stood before much honour, praises
were heaped on him. He would have become a Chief. Tell me another person
who would have exposed his soul for all the eyes to peck at.' He paused and let
his eyes linger on Mumbi. Then he looked away and said, 'Remember that few
people in that meeting are fit to lift a stone against that man. Not unless I – we –
too – in turn open our hearts naked for the world to look at.' (p. 202)

Uhuru Day becomes a solemn day for the people of Thabai. A hero's
career is surveyed and found wanting; through him the revolution was
betrayed. So, too, General R. surveys the causes and achievement of the
independence movement. He finds that the revolution has been betrayed:

'You ask why we fought, why we lived in the forest with wild beasts. You ask
why we killed and spilt blood.
'The whiteman went in cars. He lived in a big house. His children went to
school. But who tilled the soil on which grew coffee, tea, pyrethrum, and sisal?
Who dug the roads and paid the taxes? The whiteman lived on our land. He ate
what we grew and cooked. And even the crumbs from the table, he threw to his
dogs. That is why we went into the forest. He who was not on our side, was
against us. That is why we killed our black brothers. Because, inside, they were
whitemen. And I know even now this war is not ended. We get Uhuru today.
Tomorrow we shall ask: where is the land? Where is the food? Where are the
schools? Let therefore these things be done now, for we do not want another
war ... no more blood in my ... in these our hands ... ' (pp. 191–2)

We recall the epigraph to the novel where Ngugi writes:

the situation and the problems are real – sometimes too painfully real for the
peasants who fought the British yet who now see all that they fought for being
put on one side. (p. vi)

Ngugi explores at great depth the many ills the flesh and soul are heirs to. The novel closes with the problems in the lives of the principal protagonists resolved – their tension, conflicts, doubts and guilt (except Karanja's) allayed. Ngugi looks backwards to colonial times when he examines the motives of the white colonizers – embodied in the series of naive assumptions held by John Thompson on the superiority of British civilization – which in turn bring about the independence war. And as he looks ahead in a sad and, like General R., bewildered way, he asks what the sacrifice in battle has really produced, what Uhuru really means. General R.'s speech offers a gloomy forecast of the future as well as a recognition of another kind of betrayal of Kenya by Kenyans, in a speech that anticipates the subject-matter of *Petals of Blood*. This line of thought is followed by Wambui as she, Mumbi, and Warui meditate on the meaning of Mugo's last action and this in relation to their experience of the emergency, as they recall it on Uhuru Day:

> Wambui sat on and watched the drizzle and the grey mist for a few minutes. Darkness was creeping into the hut. Wambui was lost in a solid consciousness of a terrible anti-climax to her activities in the fight for freedom. Perhaps we should not have tried him, she muttered. (p. 210)

But for Ngugi, affirmation of life is what matters and affirmation is found with the people, those who by his subsequent writing – *Petals of Blood*, *Dedan Kimathi* and *Ngaahika Ndeenda* – he seeks to rally once again to challenge the new enemy. Wambui and Mumbi stand for this spirit in their simple yet certain affirmation of life:

> 'I must go now. I'm sure the fire is ready at home. Perhaps we should not worry too much about the meeting . . . or . . . about Mugo. We have got to live.'
> 'Yes, we have the village to build,' Warui agreed.
> 'And the market tomorrow, and the fields to dig and cultivate ready for the next season,' observed Wambui, her eyes trying to see beyond the drizzle and the mist.
> 'And children to look after,' finished Mumbi as she stood up and took her rain-sack ready to leave. Then suddenly she turned round and looked at the two old people, as at aged wisdom which could tell youth the secrets of life and happiness. (p. 210)

A Grain of Wheat is Ngugi's artistic tribute to the actions of the freedom fighters of the independence movement as these are represented to us through the activities of Kihika and in the various speeches that establish the legitimacy of the quest for a return of the land to the people of Kenya. The novel is a warning too, against the betrayal of the revolution in the figure of the MP who steals the land of Mr Burton from Gikonyo who wished to use it for purposes of co-operative farming.

Perhaps, too, in light of what is revealed in *Petals of Blood* there is a warning in the activities of Gikonyo since he is well on the way to being an entrepreneur capitalist who wins his living by exploiting the needs of his community. The MP is despicable – but it is perhaps a matter of one thief beating another while the majority of people look on. That majority does not emerge here, except in passive terms, as they experience the difficulties, sometimes mounting to horror of the emergency, as they gather to listen to speeches.

Gikonyo, Mugo, Karanja and Mumbi are to some extent representatives and they are found wanting. Their interest is not in politics but rather in hanging on to life and in settling the affairs of the heart. Mugo, the one of the four with positive notions of what service might consist of, is denied the chance to act because of his fallible soul. He learns too late the lesson of participation.

The novel, while it is concerned to show necessity for and the cost of getting independence, speculates little on the ways in which that independence must be used. General R.'s summary of the motives of the independence fighters provides a sort of motto for *Petals of Blood*. *A Grain of Wheat* is not a political novel in the fullest sense. The political theme is balanced against the exploration of human fallibility the novel offers. Ngugi's humanism, revealed by his care for his people and his understanding of what prompts them to action, dominates the novel.

REFERENCES AND NOTES

1. *Vide* p. 17; p. 19-21.
2. I Corinthians 15:36.
3. Exodus 3:7.
4. Ngugi wa Thiong'o, *The River Between* (London: Heinemann Educational Books, 1965, reset 1975), p. 119.

5 *Secret Lives*

▼▼▼▼▼▼▼▼▼▼▼▼▼▼▼▼▼▼▼▼▼▼▼▼▼▼▼▼▼▼▼▼▼

Because it is a systematic negation of the other person and a furious determination to deny the other person all attributes of humanity, colonialism forces the people it dominates to ask themselves the question constantly: 'In reality, who am I?'

Frantz Fanon

NGUGI writes in the preface of *Secret Lives* that the stories form his creative autobiography, that they touch on ideas and moods that affected him at the same time he was writing the novels and that his writing in general is 'an attempt to understand myself and my situation in society and in history'. There is a good deal of overlapping between the novels and the short stories in terms of theme and character. Often the short stories have characters, incidents and plots that have their counterparts in the novels or represent variant treatments of the same incidents and characters in the larger works. Ngugi accounts for the similarities with this statement:

> I think short stories are a form in themselves. I don't really think I am particularly good at them, myself. You see, you cannot really separate your moods or your preoccupations if you write in a certain period. If you write a short story and then a play and a novel at about the same time, you will find that they tend to be preoccupied with the same kind of things. That's why you find that some of the themes that are in my plays or short stories in a certain period reappear in the novel. It's not really something which one thinks about – it happens. A short story is not like an experiment, not like a visual artist might draw a sketch of something he is going to use later on. For me, when I write a short story, I want it to be as good a short story as possible when I'm writing it. Later, I may want to return to the same theme in a novel or a play. When I feel I've not exhausted that particular theme.[1]

The themes one finds in the stories and the order he imposes on them in the collection reflect Ngugi's development as a novelist: the treatments become progressively more contemporary. The stories deal with the nature and moral worth of various aspects of original Gikuyu culture, of the effect of Christian teaching both in schools and the churches on the quality of African life; of the development of capitalism, class-consciousness and human alienation as a new Kenya develops out of the independence struggle. Ngugi's position in the stories as in *A Grain of Wheat* and *Petals of Blood* is that of a humane socialist whose stories provide an account seen over the perspective of probably fifty years of relations between individuals, usually two, in a world of moral, ethical and religious uncertitude. Political Africa, in the widest sense, is the background to the stories, and what happens to the characters in the stories can be taken as a metaphor of what is happening in the land.

The first three stories in the book, as the title Ngugi gives to the section implies, tell of relations between mothers and children. The first two stories, 'Mugumo' and 'And the Rain Came Down!', tell of women who are childless and embittered because of it. Mukami is the youngest of Muthoga's four wives. She has been the favourite until it is discovered that she is barren. No longer able to bear his bitter beatings and the scorn of the other wives, she leaves in the dead of night. Passing through a grove where the dead are thrown and in despair, she invokes the spirit of the living and the dead, Murungu and Mother Earth to carry her off:

> Suddenly, as if in answer to her invocations, she heard a distant, mournful sound, pathetic yet real. The wind began to blow wildly and the last star that had so strangely comforted her vanished. She was alone in the gloom of the forest! Something cold and lifeless touched her. She jumped and at last did what the beating could not make her do – she screamed. The whole forest echoed with her scream. Naked fear now gripped her; she shook all over. And she realized that she was not alone. Here and there she saw a thousand eyes that glowed intermittently along the stream, while she felt herself being pushed to and fro by many invisible hands. (p. 6)

In her terror she finds sanctuary under the 'Sacred Mugumo – the altar of all-seeing Murungu'. There she falls asleep and has a dream vision of Gikuyu and Mumbi, 'Mother of the Nation'. She awakes, restored, determined to return to her husband and home. She has learned from Mumbi the lesson that for strength there must be unity in the family. To secure the point Mumbi has made Mukami pregnant in the arbour of Mugumo.

In the association of Gikuyu and Mumbi with Adam and Eve, the occasion of the immaculate conception in the arbour of the fig tree, in the language he employs, Ngugi exploits the similarities between Gikuyu and Christian legends and strengthens the points of his story – that strength comes from unity, from a compassionate understanding and from tolerance and co-operation. When these qualities in human relations disappear, the result is social and moral chaos. Drawing on legends from the past to make a comment on the present Ngugi offers implicitly a plea for a return to basic human values.

'And the Rain Came Down!', the second story, tells of an incident in the life of Nyokabi, who, like Mukami, is *thata* and embittered. Children have been the centre of her hopes and plans and because Murungu has not answered her plea, she reflects on the ironic forecast of her present state in a rhyme her mother chanted to her as a child:

A woman without a child, a child,
Must needs feel weary, a-weary.
A woman without a child must lonely be,
So God forgive her! (p. 10)

Suddenly driven by a 'Thing' which wells up in her, she flees the village like a creature possessed, avoiding human contact. The darkening, thunderous sky reflects her own black mood. She is caught in a sudden storm and turns for home. But she hears the cry of a child, lost in the bush. So bleak is her soul that she would ignore the cry, but the rain, pelting suddenly fiercely against her, will not let her. It drives her back till she retrieves the child. And the effect is miraculous:

But, oh, the warmth! The sweet revitalizing warmth that flows from one stream of life into another! Nyokabi's blood thawed and danced in her veins. She gained renewed hope and faith as she went up, treading dangerously over the slippery ground. She cried, 'Let me save him. Give me time, oh Murungu, to save him. Then let me die!' The rain seemed not to heed her prayer or to pity her because of her additional weight. She had to fight it out alone. But her renewed faith in living gave her strength and she was nearing the top when she slipped off the ground and fell. She woke up, undaunted, ready for the struggle. What did it matter if the child was not hers? Had the child not given her warmth, a warmth that rekindled her cold heart? So she fought on, the child clinging to her for protection. Literally dragging her legs along, she reached the top. Then the rain stopped. (p. 13)

Her act of heroism instils pride in her husband, but the lesson she learns engenders acceptance and, we presume, wins her back the love of the village.

'Gone with the Drought' tells of a time of severe drought in the land and of the young narrator's concern for an old woman of the village who is thought by most to be mad. But there is something in her eyes that suggests not madness, but mystery and knowledge. Out of concern for her he takes food, a scarce commodity in the drought, and thus he learns her story – how all her children have been taken from her in other times of drought, of her sad quest for food to save these children whom she watched die, unable to help them. When the rains break, harbingers of a good harvest, the young hero returns to the woman's hut but finds her dying. In her delirium she sees her children now waiting for her at the gate. He sees as well the food he has taken to her, unconsumed, husbanded against the great need. Ironically, she has saved the food for her children.

In showing the events, and in conveying the emotions through the experiences of the child, Ngugi teaches a lesson in tolerance compounded of pity, compassion and love which can only be learned with this force by a child.

The stories in the second part of the book treat of events in the period defined by the coming of the white man through to his departure from Kenya. In these seven stories we find a number of familiar faces, both black and white, in circumstances strongly reminiscent of the novels. Ngugi focuses his attention on the secret lives of characters in circumstances which produce a good deal more tension than in the first group. This is because two worlds come into collision in the situations.

Decent values, usually associated with original African values, suffer as a result of coming into contact with imported ones. The irony which informs the stories in this group proceeds from human relations and is not, as was the case in the first group, the irony of fate (or of magic). It is a mordant irony moving toward the scathing irony Ngugi adopts in the third and final section.

'The Village Priest' and 'The Black Bird', the first two stories of Part II – 'Fighters and Martyrs' – deal with aspects of the contact between Christianity and Gikuyu religion.

'The Village Priest' is Joshua who, at a time of drought, learns the lesson of the 'contrite heart and true' when he denies his God. He is a zealous Christian but his understanding of his faith is simplistic. Why when he prays for rain does God not send it? Why when the village rain-maker demands rain does it come down? What has he done wrong?

Confounded by his attempt to understand he decides he must appease the 'God of Agikuyu, God of my people . . . ' He visits the sacred grove of the Gikuyu God and there is confronted by the village rain-maker:

'Hmm! So the whiteman's dog comes to the lion's den. Ha! Ha! So Joshua comes to make peace. Ha! Ha! Ha! I knew you would come to me Joshua . . . You have brought division into this land in your service to the white strangers. Now you can only be cleansed by the power of your people.' (p. 25)

Ngugi shows the psychological humiliation which Joshua undergoes – the 'shame . . . [the] utter hollowness and hopelessness that can come only to a strong-willed man who has sacrificed his convictions' (pp. 25–6).

In 'The Black Bird', Mangara sacrifices a promising career in medicine, the love of a beautiful and faithful woman, and his life, to lay the curse placed on his family by 'the Black Bird'. The Black Bird is the avenging spirit of a village magician who lived at the time of Mangara's grandfather. Mangara tells his schoolboy friend, the narrator of the story, of how his grandfather in uncompromising ruthless Christian zeal had destroyed the possessions of the magician, Mundu, seeing in them and in his work the embodiments of evil, the way to eternal damnation. But it is the grandfather and his heirs who find damnation and are made martyrs to the grandfather's strict beliefs. Swearing to avenge himself the old man returns to earth as a Black Bird and later takes his revenge on Mangara's grandfather, father and mother. Mangara knows his time will come and he wears a haunted look until he finds a way to appease the avenging spirit. He is found dead under the sacred tree, Mugumo:

> His eyes wore a strange look of peace, you know, as if he had accomplished a difficult task. The look you sometimes see in the revivalists. (p. 38)

The irony is that the generations succeed each other in assuming the responsibility of their forebears. Ngugi leaves the various implications of the story to the musings of the reader. In this story he is at his least explicit.

We meet another stern Christian in 'A Meeting in the Dark'. The irony of this story is one found elsewhere in his writing – that the message of Christian love and compassion will provide a decent and upright life too often prompts the opposite behaviour. We have seen that this is so in *The River Between* and in *Petals of Blood*, in 'The Black Bird' and in subtle, less explicit ways in *Weep Not, Child* and *A Grain of Wheat*. Here we meet John, the son of a Christian preacher whose religion is arid and who, incapable of love himself, engenders only fear in his son. John is a successful pupil, well-liked and envied by everyone in his village. He is to go to Makerere College. A splendid career is about to open before him. But he has made Wakumu, a pretty and devoted village girl, pregnant. He cannot sacrifice his career for her and, so terrified is he of his father that he cannot explain his plight. Ultimately he offers Wakumu money to say someone else is responsible for her pregnancy. Appalled at his hypocrisy she refuses. He insists, fear turning him hysterical. He strangles her. 'Soon' writes Ngugi, with bitter irony, 'everyone will know that he has created and then killed.'

Ngugi understands the beliefs that have made John the moral cripple he is. But he has neither pity nor compassion for him. And this is rare in Ngugi. It accounts as well for this being the least successful of the stories.

Everything here is too pat. There are no ambiguities of character. And despite the nature of the ending, little tension. But the story does show Ngugi moving toward the creation of characters such as we find in the final three stories – the type of modern Kenyan who, through education and ambition based upon imported values, adopts a Christian name, a self-serving personal morality which is hollow at the core. John never makes it all the way through the process but figures in 'Minutes of Glory', 'Wedding at the Cross', 'A Mercedes Funeral' and 'The Mubenzi Tribesman' do.

The remaining stories in Part II deal with the emergency and post-emergency period and 'The Martyr' is the best of the three, possibly the best in the collection. Ngugi offers a microcosm of Kenya at the time of the emergency and in it we are afforded points of view which are both English and African. Mrs Hill lives on a plantation she and her husband established. She lives alone – her husband has died and her children are 'at home' in England. Castigated by her friends Mrs Smiles and Mrs Hardy, who between them purvey all the cliches associated with the white civilizing mission, Mrs Hill nevertheless prefers to treat in a kindly fashion her 'houseboy', Njoroge. She cannot know that for Njoroge she is the embodiment of those forces which have driven him from the land and forced on him the humiliation of working as a servant.

Njoroge has determined to assist the Ihii (Freedom Boys) in killing Mrs Hill, not knowing that Mrs Smiles and Mrs Hardy have told her of the murders of the Garstones, near neighbours, whose houseboy betrayed them to the same freedom fighters.

Mrs Hill muses for the time on Njoroge's loyalty – would he betray her? Njoroge, the more he considers his plan, the more divided his motives seem. His grievances are just ones. Yet he knows Mrs Hill to be a tender and loving wife and mother, qualities he values. He decides in the end to save her and runs to warn her. But she shoots him. The story of the Garstones have played on her mind and she hears in his cry of warning, betrayal.

Ngugi is dealing with the pain and shame occasioned by injustice. The irony of the story proceeds from Njoroge's reflection, as he castigates himself for going against his plan to betray Mrs Hill: 'If only he had not thought of her in human terms!' When he does he seeks to save her; when she thinks of him in human terms she has to kill him.

In 'The Return' Kamau returns to his village after his release from prison. The story is a variation of the Gikonyo-Mumbi-Karanja relationship in *A Grain of Wheat*. The difference here is that the wife, Muthoni, has believed Karanja's account that Kamau has died in prison. Muthoni was the patient sufferer, a good daughter to Kamau's parents, a faithful wife to Kamau. But then there came a child; times were very hard. Kamau's parents sanctioned her leaving with Karanja. Kamau's initial bitterness in hearing of his wife's disaffection is replaced by desolate understanding. Why should she have waited.

The story is centred in the human losses the independence struggle provoked. There was death and suffering and ultimately everyone is made into a kind of martyr.

The last story in Part II is 'Goodbye Africa'. Two unnamed expatriates prepare to leave Kenya. He resembles John Thompson and Howlands in the novels: like them he has dreamed of participating in a great civilizing mission that has gone sour. Like them during the emergency he has become bestial in his treatment of Africans, feeling in their revolutionary activities betrayal of his dream. One face haunts him in his nightmares, that of a shamba boy whom he had put to death for his insolence. In a drunken state he writes an account, a confession of his actions, by which he hopes to lay the ghostly reminder of his brutality. But fate intercedes. His wife, too, bears a guilty secret. She has had a 'fevered' love affair with an African and feels she must confess this to her husband. The irony is that the African was the shamba boy who now will return to haunt him forever. There is no hope for a new relationship to emerge as she had hoped. In a sense it will for them be impossible to say goodbye to Africa. The effect of the story is to show that their spiritual and even cultural ruthlessness is something Ngugi understands and is, ironically, analogous to the rootlessness that they and their kind through their actions foisted on Kenyans over the period of colonial history.

The last four stories are set in modern Kenya and show the consequences of historical process initiated by the introduction of modern values and methods in education, religion, and business. Ngugi's claim in 'A Mercedes Funeral' that 'Wahinya's progress from hope to a drunken despair is the story of our times' can be taken as a motto (if the adjective 'drunken' is omitted) of all the stories in Part III of the book. Each of the principal characters in the stories progress from hope to despair. Even the outwardly successful sense, in their secret hearts, that but for a trick of fate they might be in the place of the destitute and forlorn. These are stories, then, about victims and their purpose is to upbraid and castigate the new bourgeoisie, that Wabenzi tribesmen, who take on imported names and clothing, drive expensive imported cars and make victims of their own people. Ngugi's irony has a cutting edge to it: there is little ambiguity in the way he tells tales. The objects of his scorn, the objects of his pity are plain to see. Two of the stories – 'Wedding at the Cross' and

'A Mercedes Funeral' are as good examples of satiric writing as one can find in recent African writing.

The title of the first story in the section suggests the irony of the tale that is told. Beatrice, the bar girl heroine of 'Minutes of Glory' moves restlessly from bar to bar from town to town following a profession that is ill-paid, earning wages that have to be supplemented by casual prostitution. One day she tires of the poverty of her life, steals money from a sleeping, drunken lorry driver, goes into Nairobi, where she buys expensive clothing and dines well. Then she returns to the bar where she works to have a few minutes of glory before being denounced by the man from whom she has stolen. Like Wanja in *Petals of Blood*, like her friend Nyagūthīī, Beatrice flees the aridity of a loveless, Christian home. But in a world where education is a necessary qualification for any sort of a legitimate advancement she, like Wanja and Nyagūthīī, is forced into an equally loveless uncertain world. Beatrice's pitiful attempt to assert her own individuality is mocked. Paradoxically her exploiter, the rough and rejected lorry driver, becomes the centre of attention of his confrères who had formerly rejected him.

The male counterpart of Beatrice is Wahinya in 'A Mercedes Funeral'. His story is told in a bar in Ilmorog by a man whose career has had its beginnings at the same time and place as Wahinya's. The success of the narrator's life illuminates and elaborates the failure of Wahinya. For Wahinya sees, rightly, that education is the open sesame to success in modern Kenya. The proof of this is the narrator's career. He goes from one good school to another, then to Makerere where he takes a degree in commerce. From there it is an easy step to gather property and possessions and even plan a political career.

Wahinya from more or less the same starting point cannot get the schooling he wants. He works at various jobs and for a time his hopes sustain him. Eventually he becomes deeply embittered, a drunkard working in a bar, making contacts for rich men with bar girls for sexual encounters. A despised figure in life, Wahinya receives in death a prominence quite unexpected. His death coincides with an election which is being conducted in his district and his penury, which will win him despised burial, becomes the special issue in the campaign. The political campaign centred in the contest between the incumbent, a student, a farmer, and a businessman, becomes an allegory of the forces in the country which try to feast on the corpse of a dead man whose pitiable life paradoxically is the product of their own political activity. The three contestants against the incumbent, J.J.J., are a radical student and an 'intellectual worker', who campaigns on behalf of 'we workers'; an aspiring businessman who campaigns on the platform of equal business opportunities for all; and 'an ex-Government chief' who campaigns, vaguely, for an equal share of the national wealth for all.

Each, of course, stands for a point of view on potential force in the country and each has a radically different notion of what purpose the political process should serve.

The campaign culminates in an obscene parody of the decencies which normally obtain at the time of burial. Ngugi once again takes the opportunity to point out how arid and denuded is the quality of contemporary life when weighed against the past:

> Now I don't know if this be true in your area, but in our village funerals had become a society affair, our version of cocktail parties. I mean since Independence. Before 1952, you know before the Emergency, the body would be put away in puzzled silence and tears. People, you see, were awed by death. But they confronted it because they loved life. They asked: what's death? because they wanted to know what was life! They came to offer sympathy and solidarity to the living and helped in the burial. A pit. People took turns to dig it in ritual silence. Then the naked body was lowered into the earth. A little soil was first sprinkled over it. The body, the earth, the soil: what was the difference? Then came the Emergency. Guns on every side. Fathers, mothers, children, cattle, donkeys – all killed, and bodies left in the open for vultures and hyenas. Or mass burial. People became cynical about death: they were really indifferent to life. You today: me tomorrow. Why cry my Lord? Why mourn the dead? There was only one cry: for the victory of the struggle. The rest was silence. What do you think, gentlemen? Shall we ever capture that genuine respect for death in an age where money is more important than life? Today what is left? A showbiz. Status. Even poor people will run into debt to have the death of a relative announced on the radio and funeral arrangements advertised in the newspapers. And gossip, gentlemen, the gossip. How many attended the funeral? How much money was collected? What of the coffin? Was the pit cemented? Plastic flowers: plastic tears. And after a year, every year there is an Ad. addressed to the dead.

> IN LOVING MEMORY. A YEAR HAS PASSED BUT TO US IT IS JUST LIKE TODAY WHEN YOU SUDDENLY DEPARTED FROM YOUR LOVED ONES WITHOUT LETTING THEM KNOW OF YOUR LAST WISH. DEAR, YOU HAVE ALWAYS BEEN A GUIDING STAR, A STAR THAT WILL ALWAYS SHINE, etc., etc. (p. 118)|

The election campaign culminates in the funeral ceremony where the potential worth of each contestant will be judged by the grandness of the gesture he makes towards burying the corpse, consisting of the donation of money to the bereaved family and the presentation of a coffin suitable to the occasion. Ngugi's style is unadorned, without subtlety as he lays bare the cant and hypocrisy of these gestures and brings the parody to a close. The student provides a small sum of money and a simple wooden coffin and wooden cross. The farmer gives considerably more money and also a wooden coffin but one adorned with a green cow with udders and teats brimful of milk. The businessman gives considerably more money than the farmer and a coffin cut as an exact replica of the Hilton Hotel in Nairobi. J.J.J. makes the most grotesque gesture of all. His coffin 'was not a coffin at all, but really an immaculate model of a black Mercedes Benz 660S complete with doors and glasses and maroon curtains and blinds'. Wahinya, who all through his life wished to ride in a Mercedes Benz, is at last through the generosity of J.J.J. given his opportunity.

But the gesture backfires. The people see it for what it is worth:

> But somehow no applause came; not even a murmur of approval. Something had gone wrong, and we all felt it. It was like an elaborate joke that had suddenly misfired. Or as if we had all been witnesses of an indecent act on a public place. The people stood and started moving away as if they did not want to be identified with the indecency. J.J.J., his challengers and a few of their hired followers were left standing by the pit, no doubt wondering what had gone wrong. Suddenly J.J.J. returned to his own car and drove off. The others quickly left. (p. 136)

But nothing happens to change things. The people are as cynical as their masters. J.J.J. is returned to office – there is talk of a rigged election; the student returns to school, takes a degree in commerce, joins the forces of capitalism, eventually becomes a very important landlord whose estates are managed by a European firm. The businessman on the other hand becomes a victim of capitalism whose pariah-like members turn on and consume their wounded colleague. The farmer in losing the election loses everything for he has sold his prize cows, in expectation of plenty. As an MP J.J.J. saw to it that he never got his old job back as a location chief.

Ngugi is in complete control of his materials. The satire is always focused and exaggerations in character and incident are appropriate both to his theme and his craft. There appears to be no hope for a better world. The established order seeks to hold power at whatever cost and for self-seeking purposes. Education might move the masses but placed in the hands of the few it is powerless to help. The masses cannot comprehend the forces which dominate them. As the ending of the story shows the future is in the hands of the narrator of the tale:

> J.J.J. still rides in a Mercedes Benz – this time 660S – just like mine – and looks at me with well, suspicion! Four years from now . . . you never know.
> Gentlemen . . . how about one for the road? (p. 137)

Though the environment is the same in 'The Mubenzi Tribesman', it is about quite a different person – educated, for a time successful, he has extended his credit in an attempt to keep up with his 'tribesmen'. He has 'borrowed' his company's money, is caught and sent to prison. We meet him when he has just left prison, rancid with the smell of prison on him, picking his way through the festering slums where roasting goat meat sizzles next to overflowing bucket lavatories, where he will not be spotted by his 'tribesmen'. As he makes his way home to his wife, Ruth, he recalls the events in his life which culminate in his release from prison. Ngugi reveals a familiar story – the nameless hero is the only boy from his village to get a college education. At college he meets his wife, the daughter of wealthy parents. They marry. Things begin to go wrong shortly after the marriage – the money they gain from teaching is not enough to meet their financial needs – two cars, house rent, imported food and clothing. They repudiate their obligations to his family. Eventually he steals the money and does a term in prison. When he arrives home he finds Ruth coarsened and brutalized, no longer the college beauty he married. She rejects him, threatening to call the police if he fails to leave.

Ngugi depicts a society where decent optimism is replaced by brutal self-interest, without love, idealism, honesty – a society with no moral base.

'Wedding at the Cross', the fourth of the stories in Part III of the book is an allegory of modern Kenya. The elements in the story are familiar. The daughter of a sanctimonious Christian family, Miriamu, responds to the gaiety and spontaneity of Wariuki, a penurious milkman. When their love is known the father, Douglas Jones, summons Wariuki to tea to discuss the possibility of marriage to his daughter, but really to humiliate him. He does this with understated ease, so stinging Wariuki that he flees the village. But Miriamu, an independent spirit, follows him and stands by him as over the years, through hard work and single-minded purpose, Wariuki proceeds from pyrethrum picker, to milk clerk, to timber worker, to soldier with campaigns in Egypt, Palestine, Burma and Madagascar – to petty trader. He survives the Mau Mau by co-operating with the colonial regime and as his people are taken from their lands, he acquires some of it. As independence approaches he uses a loan gained from retiring expatriates to set himself up as a timber merchant. He prospers and becomes rich. He joins the Christian church in gratitude. He 'dragged' Miriamu into it, and together they become exemplary church-goers. He becomes the sort of Christian his father-in-law is and in her heart Miriamu mourns the disappearance of Wariuki who adopts the name Dodge W. Livingstone, Jr.

Wariuki's heart has festered through the years with the humiliation suffered at the hands of Miriamu's father. Dodge W. Livingstone will have revenge, but as the years pass his perspective shifts:

> Not that he was angry with Jones: the old man had been right, of course. He could not imagine himself giving his own daughter to such a ragamuffin of an upstart clerk. Still he wanted that interview erased from memory forever. And suddenly, and again he saw in that revelation the hand of God, he knew the answer. He trembled a little. Why had he not thought of it earlier? He had a long intimate conversation with his father-in-law and then made the proposal. Wedding at the cross. A renewal of the old. Douglas Jones immediately consented. His son had become a true believer. But Miriamu could not see any sense in the scheme. She was ageing. And the Lord had blessed her with two sons. Where was the sin in that? Again they all fell on her. A proper wedding at the cross of Jesus would make their lives complete. Her resistance was broken. They all praised the Lord. God worked in mysterious ways, his wonders to perform. (p. 109)

But when called upon, at the renewal ceremony, to accept 'this man' for a husband, Miriamu repudiates him:

> The vision had come back . . . At the cross, at the cross where I found the Lord . . . she saw Wariuki standing before her even as he used to be in Molo. He rode a bicycle: he was playing his tricks before a huge crowd of respectful worshippers . . . At the cross, at the cross where I found the Lord . . . he was doing it for her . . . he had singled only her out of the thrilling throng . . . of this she was certain . . . came the dancing and she was even more certain of his love . . . He was doing it for her. Lord, I have been loved once . . . once . . . I have been loved, Lord . . . And those moments in Ilmorog forest and woods were part of her: what a moaning, oh, Lord what a moaning . . . and the drums and the tambourines were now moaning in her dancing heart. She was truly Miriamu. She felt so powerful and strong and raised her head even more proudly; . . . and the priest was almost shouting: 'Do you Miriamu . . . ' The crowd waited. She looked at Livingstone, she looked at her father, and she could not see any difference between them. Her voice came in a loud whisper: 'No.' (pp. 11–12)

Ngugi's stories, in the final section of the volume, are centred in the human losses that follow in the wake of modernization that produces both cultural and spiritual rootlessness in the characters, none of whom is able to make a satisfactory response to life. All of these people are victims, though not all of them have yet found it out.

Ngugi's statement that 'I don't think I'm particularly good' at writing short stories shows shrewdness of judgement. There is some unevenness in the treatment, the ironic endings do not always succeed and some of the stories lack tension, thus interest. At times there is bad writing – a curious use of English idiom and sometimes grammar that cannot be deliberate. But for the most part the narrative line is always clear, the characteriz- ation – whether realistically or symbolically created – precisely observed and sharply portrayed. Except in one or two cases a decisive climactic moment is achieved. Moreover, the stories, because of their correspondence with events and characters in the novel, serve to elaborate the larger works and intensify the artistic purposes of their creation. Ngugi is concerned with the new Africa – with the quality of life in the here and now. And while he portrays the past as a time of unity of sensibility, he does so without sentimentality or nostalgia. If his contemporary landscape is bleak and without hope at least he has given his readers the materials with which to contemplate it through an honest rendering, both in physical and emotional terms.

REFERENCES AND NOTES

1. Reinhard Sander and Ian Munro, 'Tolstoy in Africa', *Ba Shiru*, vol. 5 (1973), p. 25.

6 *The Trial of Dedan Kimathi*

▼▼▼▼▼▼▼▼▼▼▼▼▼▼▼▼▼▼▼▼▼▼▼▼▼▼▼▼▼▼▼▼

The duty of those at the head of the movement is to have the masses behind them. Allegiance presupposes awareness and understanding of the mission which has to be fulfilled; in short, an intellectual position, however embryonic. We must not voodoo the people, nor dissolve them in emotion and confusion. Only those underdeveloped countries led by revolutionary élite who have come up from the people can today allow the entry of the masses upon the scene of history.

Frantz Fanon

DEDAN KIMATHI fought for the total liberation of the Kenya people from foreign domination and oppression. He did not achieve this in his lifetime: the struggle continues and Kimathi is the legitimate hero of the revolution. Ngugi and his colleague Micere Githae Mugo have collaborated in writing a play with a number of specific purposes. It is a 'song of praise' for the feats of leadership and resistance of the most brilliant of the generals of the independence struggle who, along with his brothers in arms, Koitalel and Me Kitilili, for example, are neglected, often repudiated heroes, their deeds for the most part not known by the present generation of young Kenyans. (The authors record in the preface their own quest for information to fill out their own sketchy knowledge.) The play is an attempt to restore the character of Kimathi to his legitimate place in the history of Kenya.

Secondly, the play establishes the connection with the masses in the present struggle by reasserting Kimathi's values. More than this the play is a self-conscious assertion of the part that literature should play in the revolution. From the preface of the play we learn the following:

> We agreed that the most important thing was for us to reconstruct imaginatively our history, envisioning the world of the Mau Mau and Kimathi in terms of the peasants' and workers' struggle before and after constitutional independence. The play is *not* a reproduction of the farcical 'trial' at Nyeri. *It is rather an imaginative recreation and interpretation of the collective will of the*

Kenyan peasants and workers in their refusal to break under sixty years of colonial torture and ruthless oppression by the British ruling classes and their continued determination to resist exploitation, oppression and new forms of enslavement. (Italics author's) (p. viii)

and further:

There was no single historical work written by a Kenyan telling of the grandeur of the heroic resistance of Kenyan people fighting foreign forces of exploitation and domination, a resistance movement whose history goes back to the 15th and 16th centuries when Kenyans and other East African people first took up arms against European colonial power – the Portuguese forces of conquest, murder and plunder. Our historians, our political scientists, and even some of our literary figures, were too busy spewing out, elaborating and trying to document the same colonial myths which had it that Kenyan people tradition-ally wandered aimlessly from place to place engaging in purposeless warfare; that the people readily accommodated themselves to the British forces of occupation! For whose benefit were these intellectuals writing? Unashamedly, some were outright defenders of Imperialism and lauded the pronouncements of colonial governors, basking in the sunshine of their pax-Anglo-Africana Commonwealths. (p. vi)

The authors present a play in which time past and time present are made to merge in a continuous present where Kimathi on trial in Nyeri and the mythic Kimathi who stands in the dock in the present tense debate the causes and prosecution of the continuing revolutionary struggle. Ngugi and his colleague state in their notes that 'the action should on the whole be seen as breaking the barrier between formal and infinite time, so that past and future and present flow into one another. The scenes (street, cell, courtroom) should also flow into one another' (p. 2).

The authors achieve their purpose by employing a number of theatrical techniques and characteristics of the non-naturalistic theatre. The play, which has an Opening, Three Movements and fourteen scenes, makes use of mime, dancing, drumming, singing, music, sudden blackouts and artful changes in lighting. The authors further enhance the suggestion of a time continuum by creating characters whose conduct in time past is coincident with their current values and motives. Moreover, the charac-ters are typed. There is nothing introspective about them. Positions have been adopted and in the play they are debated and put on trial. Further, the authors employ language in such a way to bridge the gap in time. Kimathi, for example, speaks a revolutionary language appropriate to his role in both past and present, but the vocabulary in scenes devoted to past time often uses a language, inappropriate to the past time period, drawn from revolutionary rhetoric of contemporary time which is nevertheless effective in suggesting coincidence of the struggle.

The action of the play takes place in a courtroom, on the street outside the courthouse, and in a jail cell. Charges against Kimathi are laid at the Opening and become *leitmotifs* in the play, reiterated at crucial moments as Kimathi is submitted to four trials in the main movement of the play. The dialogue between Kimathi and his accusers in the courtroom and the jail cells, is balanced by a sub-plot which describes the attempts of a Woman and later a Boy and Girl, to rescue Kimathi from prison. The two plots merge at the play's close where, when final judgement is passed on Kimathi at the close of the formal trial, the rescue attempt is in a figurative sense effected and the spirit of Kimathi is released among the people.

The action of the Three Movements moves backwards and forwards in time and place. A wide variety of characters and themes related to Kimathi and his past life, and in the present all witnesses to and participates in the historic action the play dramatizes, appear. But the general movement of the play is forward from the period of the Mau Mau independence struggle to the present, and while the penultimate scene of the play is Kimathi's forest camp at the height of the emergency, the action, the strategy discussed and the values expounded secure the relevance of the play to contemporary revolutionary movements.

We begin with a mimed enactment of the Black Man's history, which projects the action into the future:

Phase I: An exchange between a rich-looking black chief and a white hungry-looking slave trader. Several strong black men and a few women are given away for a long, posh piece of cloth and a heap of trinkets.
Bereaved relations and children weep, throwing themselves onto the ground, while others raise closed fists in a threatening manner.

Phase II: A chain of exhausted slaves, roped onto one another, drag themselves through the auditorium, carrying heavy burdens, ending up on the stage. They row a boat across the stage, under heavy whipping.

Phase III: A labour force of blacks, toiling on a plantation under the supervision of a cruel, ruthless fellow black overseer. A white master comes around and inspects the work.

Phase IV: An angry procession of defiant blacks, chanting anti-imperialist slogans through songs and thunderous shouts. (p. 5)

The First Movement conveys the tensions surrounding Kimathi's incarceration in Nyeri and dramatizes the woman's attempt to mount an escape plan for Kimathi. The Movement is mostly given over to the woman's story of Kimathi's life, as boy, as teacher and as legendary leader of his people. And in an exchange between two KAR African soldiers, the author introduces a phrase which might be taken as a motto for the play because of the manner in which it sums up the process the play delineates. One of the soldiers comments on the policy of divide and rule the authorities have fostered in the country – 'The way Mzungu makes us thirst to kill one another' – a phrase picked up by the woman who in reiterating it – 'The way the enemy makes us thirst to kill one another' – recognizes the divisiveness that is cultivated by insisting that designations and differences be maintained. The theme is examined and its implications extended in subsequent scenes as the action of the play moves from the past into the present.

Throughout the Three Movements witnesses are brought forward to accuse and to tempt Kimathi in a series of trials. 'Trials' is used here in the ambiguous sense of referring not only to the process of accusation and examination within the formal processes of the law and the informal process of torture to which Kimathi is submitted, but also to the hardship of the body and spirit that Kimathi must endure in pursuing his revolutionary objective – the difficult battle against great odds, dissension and even betrayal within his ranks, the prospect of a long, hard, soul wearying struggle.

Kimathi's first accuser appears in the Second Movement. He typifies the white settler whose speech in denouncing Kimathi as a 'mad bushwog' provides an abbreviated history of the colonial period and the paternalism which informed it:

I had cattle and sheep – by the thousands:
Where are they now?
I had acres of maize and wheat:
Where are they now?
I had a wife and daughter:
Where are they now?
Killed. Burnt. Maimed
by this lunatic and his pack of bandits.
Which innocent investor can sleep these days?
Beer and whisky are stale and bitter.
Look at me. I am no idler.
I may not be a Delamere or a Grogan
But I am a worker
I came to this country as a soldier
A simple soldier.
Fighting against banks, mortgages,
the colonial office, the whole lot
on my back.
You think it was easy?

And when I thought I would
sit down and enjoy the fruits of my labour
You struck.
I had perfect relationships with my boys
They were happy on my farm
I gave them posho, built them a school,
a dispensary ... gave them everything;
they needed
They loved me
Yes, at Olkalau they talked of
my farm with awe: loyal, meek, submissive.
Then that devil, Field Marshal, came
Milk clerk, oath clerk, murderer!
Poisoned simple minds
led astray their God-fearing souls
with his black mumbo jumbo
My wife, my daughter, my property.
Now, now, you'll die. (pp. 28–9)

His hysteria stands juxtaposed to the calm of the Judge Prosecutor who
doubles as Shaw Henderson, the Special Branch policeman who tracked
Kimathi down in the forest and arrested him. The four trial scenes which
comprise the Second Movement move the action through historical time
from the emergency period to the present and dramatize the confron-
tation between the people – peasants and workers – symbolized by
Kimathi, the Woman and the Boy and Girl, on the one hand, and the
capitalist-bourgeois epitomized by Shaw Henderson, the Bank Manager,
the Business Executive and the Priest. And while the scenes advance the
various aspects of the debate between accommodation and betrayal, the
various parts of the argument are subsumed into the fundamental
question of humanity posed in the paradoxical exchange between the
Judge and Kimathi:

JUDGE: There is no liberty without law and order.
KIMATHI: There is no order and law without liberty. (p. 27)

The law which will try Kimathi is a foreign law, one in which he had no
hand in the making, a law compounded of two parts, the first of which has
in the past and will continue into the present to 'protect the man of
property, the man of wealth, the foreign exploiter', the other half of
which, serving the needs of finance capitalism, 'silences the poor, the
hungry, our people'. Kimathi repudiates the form of justice he will
experience:

I despise your laws and your courts. What have
they done for our people?
What?

Protected the oppressor. Licensed the murderers
of the people: Our people,
whipped when they did not pick your tea leaves
your coffee beans
Imprisoned when they refused to 'ayah'
your babies
and 'boy' your houses and gardens
Murdered when they didn't rickshaw
your ladies and your gentlemen.
I recognize only one law, one court:
the court and the law of those who
fight against exploitation,
The toilers armed to say
We demand our freedom.
That's the eternal law of the oppressed,
of the humiliated, of the injured, the insulted! (pp. 26–7)

Kimathi is now submitted to a number of examinations and temptations by Henderson, a realist who acts out of self-interest and who can adjust with cynical ease to new accommodations. But he projects the white settler's point of view and interest as these stand the time frame suggested by the play. 'Nations live by strength and self-interest', he says to Kimathi and any action which serves those ends are cannibal. Henderson offers Kimathi his life for a confession of guilt which would effectively destroy the revolution. But Kimathi's mission has been 'to protect the struggle from betrayal, opportunism, and regional chauvinism' and he repudiates Henderson's offer, eventually driving him to a rage which causes him to inflict torture on Kimathi.

Kimathi is now tempted in turn by the Banker, Business Executive and Priest, each the hireling of international finance capitalism and each an agent of betrayal, opportunism and regional chauvinism. The exchange between the Banker, for example, reveals that new forms of exploitation create familiar kinds of oppression. Appealing to Kimathi to recant, the Banker advances justification for a continuance of the status quo:

BANKER: Listen. We are now prepared to settle for a black man's government. In partnership Only . . .

KIMATHI: Only?

BANKER: Confess, Repent. Plead guilty. Co-operate – like the surrendered generals. Tell your people to come out of the Forest. We need stability. There never can be progress without stability. Then we can finance big Hotels . . . International Hotels . . . Seaside resorts . . . Night Clubs . . . Casinos . . . Tarmac roads . . . oil refineries and pipelines . . . Then tourists from USA, Germany, France, Switzerland, Japan, will flock in. Investment, my friend, development, prosperity, happiness.

KIMATHI: And my people?

BANKER: Who are your people?

KIMATHI: The oppressed of the land ... all those whose labour power has transformed this land. For it is not true that it was your money that built this country. It was our sweat. It was our hands. Where do our people come in in your partnership for progress?

BANKER: Toilers there will always be. Even in America, England, France, Germany, Switzerland, Sweden, Japan ... all the civilized world. There are servants and masters ... sellers of labour and buyers of labour. Masters and servants.

INDIAN: True! True! Even in holy religion ... there are workers ... Brahmins and untouchables.

KIMATHI: The religion of enslavement! Like colonialism which makes the colonized sweat and bleed while master comes to harvest.

BANKER: Racialism ... No. Colour Bar ... No. This may have been necessary in the 1930s. But now with more and more educated black people (*points at the African who nods*) there's obviously no need for colour discrimination. We have grown wiser.

INDIAN: True! True!

KIMATHI: Money ... for a sell-out of our people ... NEVER. (pp. 39–40)

The Business Executive, the next tempter, reveals the same paucity of vision for the future, the same cynical self-interest as he expounds 'Capital partnership in Capital progress' for independent Kenya:

There have been two important announcements. They have said: No more racialism. No more colour bar. In public places. In administration. In business. In the allocation of loans. In the grabbing, well, in the acquisition of land. Partnership in progress, that's the new motto. Is this not what we have been fighting for? Any black man who now works hard and has capital can make it to the top. We can become local directors of foreign companies. We can now buy land in the White Highlands. White Highlands no more. It's now: willing Seller, willing Buyer. (p. 45)

But for Kimathi, the partnership, based on the acquisition of capital property, implies selling his people into a second slavery:

Partnership in Progress. Towards what end?
What will you do to the widows, orphans, the labouring millions? New masters. We labour for you, pick coffee and tea for you. Is that why poor men died and

continue to die in the forests? General Kago, Baimunge, Matenjagwo . . . and many brave sons are still locked in there . . . Stanley Mathenge . . . (p. 47)

The cant and hypocrisy of the fourth tempter, the Priest, is denounced with scathing accuracy by Kimathi. He is the spiritual ally of the exploitation foisted on the masses by colonialism and capitalism over the historical span. Kimathi outwits him at his own dialectical game. The Priest seeks to divert the people from contemplating their impoverished condition with spiritual abstractions. Referring to passages marked by Kimathi in his own Bible –

> So I returned, and considered all the oppressions that are done under the sun: and behold the tears of such as were oppressed, and they had no comforter; and on the side of their oppressors there was power; but they had no comforter. Why? (p. 48)

– the Priest asserts that the struggle is not an earthly struggle but a spiritual one, 'God and Satan locked in an immortal struggle for the domination of our soul' and enjoins Kimathi to give his soul to Jesus: 'Jesus will never betray you'. For Kimathi this represents betrayal:

> KIMATHI: Betrayal. Betrayal. Prophets. Seers. Strange. I have always been suspicious of those who would preach cold peace in the face of violence. Turn the other cheek. Don't struggle against those that clothe themselves as butterflies. Collaborators.
>
> PRIEST: Surrender your heart, Dedan. Let Jesus speak to you today.
>
> KIMATHI: (*continuing his speech as it were*): I have spoken with the God of my ancestors in dreams and on the mountain and not once did he counsel me to barter for my soul. (p. 49)

The scenes with the four accusers – tempters – give the authors the opportunity to display the Judas-like enemies of the people. Kimathi withstands their suits with a resolve as firm as their betrayals are blatant. His greatest struggle is with himself. Kimathi's long speech in the penultimate scene of the play, a scene which sums up the experiences of the guerilla fighters in the emergency period, provides lessons for future struggles. The treachery of Wambararia, Kimathi's brother, symbolizes the potential for betrayal in all popular revolutionary movements. And Kimathi's agony over the soul recognizes the need that:

> We shall continue to suffer
> Until that day
> We can recognize our own
> Our true kinsman
> When we can correctly

Identify our enemies
What is this superstition about
Kindred blood even when it
Turns sour and treacherous
To our long cherished cause? ... (pp. 73–4)

and a further need to:

... learn from our past strength
Past weaknesses
From past defeats
And past victories.
Also clear a few farms to grow grain
Here in the Forest
Where we have even made friends with
Birds and snakes and animals
So that they even warn us
About enemies approaching
Here we must plant seeds for a
future society
Here in the forest armed in body
mind and soul
We must kill the lie
That black people never invented anything
Lay forever to rest that inferiority
complex
Implanted in our minds by centuries
of oppression.
Rise, Rise workers and peasants of Kenya
Our victory is the victory of the working
people
The victory of all those in the world
Who today fight and struggle for total
liberation. (p. 68)

Thus the connection between the struggle of the Kenyan people and
with other revolutionary people is suggested throughout the play.

Kimathi, then, is the revolutionary leader, the voice of the people in
whom symbolically is summed up the unwitting aspirations of the
suppressed masses and their potential for revolutionary action.

In the play Kimathi is in the dock. But the overall effect the play
achieves is to put the various witnesses – the Shaw Henderson generation
of settlers, the new bourgeois capitalistic exploiters, the hypocritic
churchmen – on trial for crimes against humanity and the nation itself
and on trial against future achievements. Kimathi's supporters, symbolized by the Woman who leads the Boy and Girl to wisdom and courage,
represent the future potential in the nation. The play closes with an

exhortation to the working classes and peasants to become a revolutionary force. The potential for this happening is symbolized by the Boy and Girl who are in the centre of a 'mighty crowd of workers and peasants' who sing 'a thunderous freedom song', and the Boy and Girl symbolize not only the revolutionary potential of the country but also the uneducated masses who need instruction of the kind the Woman gives them in the sub-plot throughout the play if the potential they possess is to be released. The authors are quite explicit about the function they mean their play to have and in this respect it is both a piece of theatre and a piece of literature:

> In this we believe that Kenyan Literature – indeed all African Literature, and its writers is on trial. We cannot stand on the fence. We are either on the side of the people or on the side of imperialism. African Literature and African Writers are either fighting with the people or aiding imperialism and the class enemies of the people. We believe that good theatre is that which is on the side of the people, that which, without masking mistakes and weaknesses, gives people courage and urges them to higher resolves in their struggle for total liberation. So the challenge was to truly depict the masses (symbolised by Kimathi) in the only historically correct perpective; positively, heroically and as the true makers of history. (pp. iv–v)

7 Petals of Blood

▼▼▼▼▼▼▼▼▼▼▼▼▼▼▼▼▼▼▼▼▼▼▼▼▼▼▼▼▼▼▼▼

In the colonial countries, the spirit of indulgence is dominant at the core of the bourgeoisie: and this is because the national bourgeoisie identifies itself with the Western bourgeoisie from whom it has learnt its lessons. It follows the Western bourgeoisie along its path of negation and decadence without ever having emulated it in its first stages of exploration and invention ... It is already senile before it has come to know the petulance, the fearlessness or the will to succeed of youth.

Frantz Fanon

THE materials of *Petals of Blood*, Ngugi's fourth novel, are related to those of the earlier novels but are more abundantly conveyed. In a novel almost double the size of *A Grain of Wheat* he widens and deepens his treatment of themes which he has narrated and dramatized before – themes related to education, both formal and informal; religion, both Christian and customary; the alienation of the land viewed from the historical point of view and as a process which continues in the present; the struggle for independence and the price paid to achieve it. And to these themes he has added artistic representation of the betrayal of the independence movement and its authors, the nature and cost of modernity as this coincides with the emergence of a Kenyan middle-class, and of the need for the creation of a cultural liberation struggle fostered by the peasants and workers. This is a political novel in the widest sense. If Ngugi's politics have become more comprehensive as novelistic statement, so, too, has his humanism. Of his purposes in writing Ngugi says:

My position here is very simple. As I said in your earlier question, I believe that a people have a right to know how wealth is produced in their country, who controls it and who benefits. I believe that every Kenyan has a right to decent housing, decent food, and decent clothing. I believe that no Kenyan should be able to sleep with any peace of mind for as long as he knows that what he is feeding upon has been taken from the mouths of the thirsty and hungry in

Kenya. I also believe that no Kenyan should be able to sleep peacefully for as long as he knows that the wealth of the country is still controlled by foreign merchants.

In other words, I believe in a national economy free from any foreign domination or free from imperialist control. These are my fairly simple beliefs and what labels are put on them is really the business of whoever is fixing the labels on these simple beliefs. In a nutshell, I would say that I believe that our national economy reflected in our national culture should be able to develop freely but that Kenyan wealth should feed, clothe, and shelter Kenyans.[1]

For Ngugi the independence movement has been betrayed and the peasant and worker for whom the war was fought have been further alienated from the land – the source of life – duped and made pitiable by a growing Kenyan middle-class of entrepreneurs in league with international finance capitalism. Ngugi is on the side of the peasants and workers. 'All writers can do is really try to point out where things are wrong', says Ngugi. 'But fiction should be firmly on the side of the oppressed. Fiction should firmly embody the aspirations and hopes of the majority – of the peasants and workers.' He says further that 'fiction cannot be the agent of change. The people are the agent of change'.[2]

The cumulative impact of the book, closing as it does with an apostrophe to the rising spirit of the workers and peasants marching forward in the struggle for liberation, is achieved by novelistic indirection. The point of view of the book is not that of the peasants and workers. Ngugi conveys a sense of their plight by presenting the lives, in both dramatic actions and through the revelations of their 'secret lives' of four disaffected and unaccommodated, highly articulate characters who come together by chance in Ilmorog.

The novel is divided into four parts – Part One: is called 'Walking'; Part Two: 'Toward Bethlehem'; Part Three: 'To Be Born' and Part Four: 'Again . . . La Luta Continua'. The story is told through a variety of narrative methods – by one or other member of the town of Ilmorog, through the recollections of one or another character, sometimes by an omniscient narrator in the first person plural 'we'. The novel adopts a variety of time frames. The present-tense actions of the novel take about ten days; the stories of the lives of the principal characters as the novel gives them to us span twelve years. But Ngugi goes backwards and forward in time, to 1896 when the exploitation of Kenya by Europeans began, and in some passages to the pre-historical period of Africa. Since his basic form is the crime thriller or detective story his technique is appropriate. What he achieves by adopting a technique of broken chronology and interrupted accounts of individual stories as these relate to the central inquiry in the novel, is a pattern of gradual revelation of incident, character, motive and psychological makeup.

The present-tense action of the book takes place over a period of about ten days. Chief Inspector Godfrey of the Kenyan Police Force conducts an investigation into the murder of three men – Kimeria, Chui and Mzigo – in New Ilmorog. Each is a businessman with investments in New Ilmorog. Each has been linked intimately – sometimes in ways they do not know – with the four principal suspects of their murders – the four principal characters in the novel – Munira, Abdulla, Wanja and Karega. The three men have been murdered in Wanja's hostelry and their bodies burned in a fire that destroys the building and injures its owner. Wanja is in hospital as Inspector Godfrey conducts his examination for discovery of the murderer among the three men, each of whom, as he knows, has motive to murder Kimeria, Chui and Mzigo. As the inquiry into the murder goes forward, so the lives of the principal participants are revealed and the strange pattern of interrelationships between the characters emerges through flashbacks thematically tied to the investigation. These flashbacks in the first instance cover the next timespan the novel presents, a period of twelve years from the time when Munira arrived at a drought-ridden old Ilmorog until Inspector Godfrey leaves New Ilmorog, the murder solved.

Murder has traditionally been a metaphor for an inquiry into the state of a nation and the health, both mental and spiritual, of the lives of its citizens. And coincidence is the hallmark of its technique. It is important to understand the complexity of the pattern of interrelationships Ngugi creates in the novel, since the unity of the novel proceeds from this. What on the surface seems a rambling book is in fact a carefully and highly unified piece of writing.

The first of the suspects is Munira. He is the village schoolmaster, the first such person to make a success of a school in the drought-ridden plain. He has seen it grow and flourish, seen new teachers added to his staff and, at the time of his arrest, sees one of his boys find a prized place in Siriana Secondary School, where Munira himself had once been a pupil, as, in fact, had all of the principal characters in the novel. Munira is the son of a wealthy, austere and very religious father, a man of 75 years of age whose life has spanned the history of modern Kenya. Munira, seen alongside the wealthy father and brothers and sisters who have made a successful entry into the middle-classes, is judged and judges himself a failure. Moreover, he has married a frigid Christian woman. His life has been characterized by an unsuccessful search for the means to overcome his failure. He escapes to Ilmorog, a derelict town, where only a few peasants frequent the bar owned by Abdulla, where children attended school in a willy-nilly fashion. Munira fears connection and involvement with people and the paucity of his life is revealed even in his teaching. In one scene Ngugi has him take his pupils into the fields to study nature:

'Look. A flower with petals of blood.' (p. 21)

Munira stifles the poetry in the child's imagination:

'There is no colour called blood. What you mean is that it is red. You see? You must learn the names of the seven colours of the rainbow. Flowers are of different kinds, different colours. Now I want each one of you to pick a flower ... Count the number of petals and pistils and show me its pollen ... ' (p. 21)

In like manner he cannot answer the questions the children asked about fundamental aspects of life, as education provokes them to try and understand:

What was a law? What was nature? Was he a man? Was he God? A law was simply a law and nature was nature. What about men and God? Children, he told them, it's time for a break. Man ... law ... God ... nature: he had never thought deeply about these things and he swore that he would never again take the children to the fields. Enclosed in the four walls he was the master, aloof, dispensing knowledge to a concentration of faces looking up to him. There he could avoid being drawn in ... (p. 22)

The second of the detainees is Abdulla, the son of an African mother and Indian father. Abdulla has been a freedom fighter in the independence war and has lost a leg in the struggle. The rewards of the independence he expected to have do not come his way. He returns to his home and for a time wins a living with a donkey cart. Eventually embittered and betrayed by the growing number of Kenyan middle-class landlords, he travels to Ilmorog with a boy called Joseph whom he literally has salvaged from a rubbish heap. In Ilmorog he runs a *duka* and sells drinks to peasants, yells at Joseph and alternates in mood between surly silence and petulant irony, which he directs mostly at Munira and his work in the school.

Wanja is the third suspect of the murders. She comes to Ilmorog to live with her grandmother Nyakinyua on a plot of land that has traditionally belonged to her family. But she was born in Limuru, where Munira and Abdulla were also born and she has fled the area for many of the same reasons as they have. The daughter of a money-grubbing father who witnesses the changes in post-independence from a farming to a cash economy, she looks for a joyous life beyond the arid home she lives in. She experiences a series of ironic reversals as she pursues her quest. As a schoolgirl she is seduced by a married man who promises her a good life but who laughingly abandons her when she becomes pregnant. She throws her new-born child down a drain and lives with the guilt of her action and the knowledge that she can never have another child. For a time she works as a barmaid, – 'not', says Ngugi, 'a prostitute, not a straight girl, her salary not regulated but paid according to the whim of the employer. She is a member of the most ruthlessly exploited category of women in Kenya'.[3]

Wanja comes to Ilmorog, to find peace in a return to the soil of her ancestors. With Munira she seeks to fulfil a prophecy of the local sage Mugo wa Mwathi that she can conceive a child at the time of the full moon. But the liaison between them is unsatisfactory. It does not produce a child and, worse, it increases the sense of alienation in each of them because of its joylessness. For Wanja Munira is the means merely of fulfilling the prophecy. And as Munira admits, he has only a carnal need for Wanja. The joylessness of his life, his inability to become involved with people is characterized by his sexual impotency.

Karega is the fourth suspect. It is through Karega and his connections with the other three figures that Ngugi cinches tight the web of coincidence he has been weaving. Karega comes to Ilmorog in search of Munira who had once been his teacher. He, too, as with the others, comes from Limuru. Karega is the younger brother of Nding'uri, a man who had fought with Abdulla in the independence movement and who had been betrayed to the British authorities by a man from his own village. Nding'uri was hanged. And though he never knew his brother, Karega learns about him from Abdulla. More than this Karega has been the lover of Munira's sister, Mukami. But their love has been denied by Munira's austere father because Karega's brother has been a Mau Mau, suspected, in fact, of cutting off the ear of the father. When the relationship is denied, Mukami drowns herself, a loss that both Karega and Munira feel deeply, a sorrow that lingers because they fail to understand the reason for her suicide, and a sorrow which eventually causes Munira to drive Karega from Ilmorog.

Karega becomes a teacher in Munira's school. And it is he who, when Ilmorog suffers a drought which threatens to kill the population, organizes a trek to Nairobi to see their absentee Member of Parliament who they believe, though in ways they but vaguely comprehend, will alleviate their stress. The journey, led by Abdulla who takes on again his former powers of command and displays his skill at bushcraft, is a success but not for the reasons they had foreseen. The MP, Nderi wa Rueri, totally misunderstands the peasant trekkers. He enjoins them to go home and to work hard. The frustration of his constituents boils over and they chase him through the streets. Ironically this attracts the notice of the press which takes up their case, as does a lawyer who devotes his life to the down-and-out in society. Charity abounds and the villagers return to Ilmorog to peace and relative comfort, to a period of calm.

It is during this period of calm that Karega and Wanja fall in love and experience a period of simple joyousness. It is during this period, too, that Nyakinyua makes Theng'eta, a distillation from a flower with 'petals of blood' that when taken soothes the body and exposes the soul. In a hallucinatory experience Karega reveals among other things his love affair with Munika and her apparent reasons for suicide. Munira, jealous of the love between Wanja and Karega, uses the involvement of the latter in the death of his sister as an excuse for having him fired from his job.

Karega leaves Ilmorog when construction begins on the trans-Africa road linking Nairobi and Ilmorog to the great cities of Africa. At about the same time a small airplane surveying for the trans-Africa road crashes in Ilmorog. The accident attracts much attention. Wanja and Abdulla sell them food and Theng'eta. Ilmorog overnight becomes famous 'well beyond the walls of the ridge and the plains'. Because of these factors, Ilmorog experiences a period of feverish growth and becomes a modern city. First a church and a police station, then investment capital – the monopoly for producing Theng'eta is taken from Wanja and a distillery owned by Chui, Kimeria and Mzigo is built to mass-produce the liquor; peasants are seduced into easy bank loans and then find their land taken from them when banks foreclose; a cultural tourist centre – Utamaduni – is created ostensibly to attract tourist dollars but in reality to serve as a centre for smuggling 'of gemstones and ivory plus animal and even human skins. It was a centre for the plunder of the country's natural and human assets' (p. 334). Wanja, no longer prepared to be exploited, becomes the prosperous madam of an Ilmorog brothel. Munira becomes first a drunkard – drinking to forget, to lose himself in an act of self-denial – and then a reformed and charismatic Christian.

Eventually Karega returns to New Ilmorog, this time to work in the Theng'eta factory and to begin to organize workers to agitate for better working conditions.

The melodrama one associates with some styles of romance thrillers informs the novel's close. Wanja stabs Kimeria with a panga in her private quarters. But the fact is never discovered because the building is razed by a fire set by Munira and from which Wanja is rescued at the last moment by Abdulla who, too, planned to murder Kimeria, his and Nding'uri's betrayer. Munira, deeply jealous of Wanja's influence over Karega and in the grip of a religious fanaticism, sets fire to the brothel for the rather limp reason he gives to Inspector Godfrey – 'I – I wanted to save Karega'.

The reason is sufficient if we accept Munira as mad. But he is articulate enough throughout the novel as he writes for Inspector Godfrey a long account of his life and those events leading up to his murder.

The novel closes with Inspector Godfrey returning to Nairobi in a first-class carriage, while Karega has his failing faith in the possibility of a peasant and worker revolution renewed by a girl who comes to the prison to tell him of the organization of the Wakombozi – 'the society of one world liberation'.

The summary of the plot, of the present-time action and events in the novel, complex as it is, conveys little of the complexities of the comment and argument Ngugi makes on the politics and the place of the people in the political process, on the history of Kenya as this displays and accounts for the political situation, on the ambiguous position of education as this is being used and ought to be used in interpreting the history and shaping the political destiny of the country, on religious and secret societies as these are used to confuse and command the masses, further alienating them from their land.

Concern over the land is a central theme in the novel as it has been in the earlier ones. It is what has happened to the land, how the African has been alienated from the land first by the imperial-colonialists who helped themselves to the land, paying into the pockets of a few whatever worth they consigned to it, and subsequently by a class of African landlords who, because of their connections with the forces of world capitalism, are able to manage the purchase price, that concerns Ngugi. And it is the question of how to re-achieve the land that links the Kenyan people to struggle with other movements in the Third World. The struggle has an historic as well as contemporary dimension and more than once in the book the unity of experience and purpose is conveyed in references to 'Chaka ... Toussaint ... Samori ... Nat Turner ... Arap Manyei ... Mondlane ... Cabral ... Kimathi ... Nkrumah' and others. The fictional embodiments of these figures in *Petals of Blood* are Ole Masai and Abdulla.

What happens to Ilmorog – how it is converted from a worn out village, raped more than once in its history, to a glistening, neon-lighted new town and compared to other Kenyan towns – Nairobi, Thika, Kisumu, Nakuru – is symbolic of what the modernizing process, in the sway of development capitalism, becomes as Ngugi apprehends it:

Within only ten years – how time galloped, he thought – Ilmorog peasants had been displaced from the land: some had joined the army of workers, others were semi-workers with one foot in a plot of land and one foot in a factory, while others became petty traders in hovels and shanties they did not even own, along the Trans-Africa Road, or criminals and prostitutes who with their stolen guns and over-used cunts eked a precarious living from each and everybody – workers, peasants, factory owners, blacks, whites – indiscriminately. There were a few who tried their hands at making sufurias, karais, water tins, chicken-feeding troughs; shoemakers, carpenters; but how long would they last, seeing that they were being driven out of their trades by more organised big-scale production of the same stuff? The herdsmen had suffered a similar fate: some had died; others had been driven even further out into drier parts away from the newly enclosed game-parks for tourists, and yet others had become hired labourers on wheatfields or on farms belonging to wealthier peasants. And behind it all, as a monument to the changes, was the Trans-Africa Road and the two-storied building of the African Economic Bank Ltd. (p. 302)

And the generalized circumstances described in the passages are made vivid in the experiences of Nyakinyua to resist the bank's foreclosure on her land, the land which ultimately Wanja redeems for the loss of her business:

Nyakinyua, the old woman, tried to fight back. She tramped from hut to hut calling upon the peasants of Ilmorog to get together and fight it out. They looked at her and they shook their heads: whom would they fight now? The Government? The Banks? KCO? The Party? Nderi? Yes who would they really fight? But she tried to convince them that all these were one and that she would fight them. Her land would never be settled by strangers. There was something grand, and defiant in the woman's action – she with her failing health and flesh trying to organise the dispossessed of Ilmorog into a protest. But there was pathos in the exercise. Those whose land had not yet been taken looked nervously aloof and distant. One or two even made disparaging remarks about an old woman not quite right in the head. Others genuinely not seeing the point of a march to Ruwa-ini or to the Big City restrained her. She could not walk all the way, they told her. But she said: 'I'll go alone . . . my man fought the white man. He paid for it with his blood . . . I'll struggle against these black oppressors . . . alone . . . ' (p. 276)

In a struggle and in an assertion of the spirit such as prompts Nyakinyua to resist, will come as a means of securing a better future. Karega on his return to New Ilmorog, in seeing what has happened here – which his experience has confirmed is happening elsewhere – knows that:

Kenya, the soil, was the people's common shamba, and there was no way it could be right for a few, or a section, or a single nationality, to inherit for their sole use what was communal, any more than it would be right for a few sons and daughters to own and monopolise their father or mother. It was better for him to get reconciled to his situation: since the only thing that he had now was his two hands, he would somehow sell its creative power to whoever would buy it and then join with all the other hands in ensuring that at least they had a fair share of what their thousand sets of fingers produced. (p. 302)

Ngugi has a compassionate understanding of his other principal characters. Wanja, for example, has taken the only route open to her in her life and apart from the period of her love affair with Karega her life has been mean and miserable. She chooses to exploit rather then being exploited by the moneyed class when New Ilmorog comes into being. Ngugi imputes to Wanja a stature larger than life. She is stronger than all of those around her, survives ordeals they do not, controls, ultimately, her destiny in a way they cannot. She has been barmaid and 'madame', victim and victor. She stands for Kenyan womanhood in a number of ways – because of her experience of what happened in the country at every social level, because of her knowledge of nearly all the languages of Kenya – Gikuyu, Luo, Swahili, Kamba, and Luhya. For Abdulla she symbolizes the source of a new creative energy but more than this – in her life is seen the caprices to which such forces are submitted in the ebb and flow of history:

> Under her firm guidance, Ilmorog suddenly seemed to expand: new roads, influx of workers, banks, experts, dancers and numerous small trades and crafts. He saw the changes as something being brought about by Wanja's magic. What a woman! One in a thousand! For she seemed, to him anyway, the true centre of all the numerous activities that were working in obedience to an invisible law. Then disaster had once again come into his life just when success and victory seemed so near, within his grasp. He applauded he selfless act of honour in redeeming her family land. But he feared the effect of this on her. For suddenly it was as if she had lost that firm grasp, that harmony with the invisible law. (pp. 310–11)

She enters her career as whore-mistress frankly and honestly and accommodates herself to the new law of the land, of which her profession is a reflection:

> 'My heart is tearless about what I have committed myself to. You know I have tried. Where was I to throw these girls that were part of the old Theng'eta premises? To others who too would profit from their bodies? No, I am not doing this for their sakes. From now onwards it will always be: Wanja First. I have valued your friendship. And I hope we can remain friends. But this is my cup. I must drink it.' (pp. 311–12)

Ultimately she is returned to the position of harmonious connection with the invisible law, a connection made manifest in the drawing she makes in the hospital, a drawing that is, as it were, forced from her by will beyond herself, a will deriving from forces still alive in the country. The anticipated birth with its Messianic associations, foreshadows the apocalypse:

> Wanja got a piece of charcoal and a piece of cardboard. For one hour or so she remained completely absorbed in her sketching. And suddenly she felt lifted

out of her own self, she felt waves of emotion she had never before experienced. The figure began to take shape on the board. It was a combination of the sculpture she once saw at the lawyer's place in Nairobi and images of Kimathi in his moments of triumph and laughter and sorrow and terror – but without one limb. When it was over, she felt a tremendous calm, a kind of inner assurance of the possibilities of a new kind of power. She handed the picture to her mother.

'Who . . . who is this . . . with . . . with so much pain and suffering on his face? And why is he laughing at the same time?' (p. 338)

Wanja never denies her peasant roots, despite the various experiences she has of the world beyond the village. She gives up her business in order to save the ancestral land of her family. And in the end she conceives a child, fittingly fathered by the real hero of the book, Abdulla, proof that the possibility of future happiness and growth lies in the revolutionary spirit.

Ngugi knows, too, what has gone into the making of Munira. He, too, in the way his life has developed reveals a pattern of action and reaction, seen mostly from the religious point of view, which has shaped the sensibility of modern Kenya. Ngugi deplores the hysterical brand of charismatic evangelicalism practised by Munira in the latter third of the book, as much as he deplores the effect of more formal Christian religion. Both forms of Christianity divert people's attention away from contemplating the real nature of their circumstance and what they must do to correct this. Nevertheless, Ngugi uses Munira effectively to castigate the character whom he holds the most loathsome in the book, Munira's father. Munira's father represents for Ngugi those Kenyans who, over the years, have persistently sided with the oppressor.

Munira's father's apostasy is complete. He denies his own father and becomes a Christian because political strength and monetary reward are with the missionaries. He refuses to take the oath in support of the independence movement thus denying the legitimate claims of his countrymen. Finally he sides with the new imperialists to divide the Kenyan people. Munira's denunciation is intimidating – if a little out of character – in the political attitudes it expresses:

'And yet in 196—, after Independence, you took an oath to divide the Kenya people and to protect the wealth in the hands of only a few. What was the difference? Was an oath not an oath? Kneel down, old man, and ask the forgiveness of Christ. In heaven, in the eyes of God, there are no poor, or rich, this or that tribe, all who have repented are equal in His eyes.' (p. 341)

Ngugi has stated that some of the characters in the novel are meant more obviously to be symbols than others. All of the characters have symbolic associations but where Munira, Abdulla, Karega and Wanja are fully realized figures, resonant with ambiguities, uncertainties, contradictions, and until their tales are told, a sense of mystery, Chui, Kimeria and Mzigo, Nderi wa Rieri, Munira's father and Rev. Jerrod stand 'as class types, a typical class that has come to be completely indifferent to the cry of the people. I see no value whatever in the middle-class'.

It is important to note, as well, the added depth of meaning Ngugi achieves by the allegorical associations of the names which he gives to many of his characters. The two English names of the schoolmasters convey the allegory readily enough to the non-Kenyan reader. The Rev. Iron Monger is a man whose religion is as heated as a forge and his activity is to shape the tools which will serve God and the nation. Cambridge Fraudsham, is revealed as his name implies – perhaps too obviously as a fraud and a sham. He is the product of Cambridge, one of the two senior universities of the English-speaking world, and elite institution and the model for the élitism he practises in Siriana. It is in the African names that the full importance of the allegorical association is revealed. Munira means 'stump' and this describes his devitalized state in the novel, his inability to connect with those around him. Wanja, whose affairs are described with a sensuality more frank than those of any of the other female characters in Ngugi's work, assumes such a position of influence in Ilmorog that it is assumed by the towns people that her name comes from 'Wanjiku', the mother of the nine clans of the Gikuyu people. Wanja also means 'stranger or outsider'. Similarly Karega means 'he – who – refuses', and for the way of saying an outsider and he is cast as 'archetypal non-conformist, who travels from idealistic youthful searching for a cause to the statis of of anti-establishment revolutionary leader'. 'Chui' is the Kiswahili word for 'leopard'. In African folk tales the leopard is cast as a 'shrewd, grasping, brutal tyrant-King'. The MP for Ilmorog, the Hon. Nderi wa Riera means 'vulture son of air'. Plainly he lives a 'vulture-life existence, living high above the people, fattening off their misery and feeding as his name sake on the dead and near-dead people and cattle of his constituency'. Other names, given to lesser characters in the novel point out Ngugi's attempt to establish universal character types while fixing his action in the immediate locale. Muturi means 'black' and Ruoro means 'the scar or furrow'. Njuguna represents the 'common man'. The application of allegorical names in the novel is one of several unifying devices Ngugi employs in the novel.*

---

*I am indebted to an article by Cyril Treister, published under the title 'An addition to the genre of the proletriat novel', in the *Nairobi Times* for 6 November 1978.

Ngugi's statement accounts for the presentation of the three murdered men. The writer of their obituaries, unconscious of course of the irony of the language he uses, describes Chui, Mzigo and Kimeria as:

> three well-known nationalist fighters for political, educational, and above all, economic freedom for Africans. Their ownership and management of *Theng'eta Breweries & Enterprises Ltd.*, which had brought happiness and prosperity to every home in the area as well as international fame for the country, was cited as an example of their joint entrepreneurial genius, unmatched even by the famed founders of the industrial revolution in Europe, Our Krupps, our Rockefellers, our Fords! And now their lives were brutally ended when they were engaged in a bitter struggle for the total African ownership and control of the same Theng'eta factories and their subsidiaries in other parts of the country. Negotiations for them to buy out the remaining shares held by foreigners were soon to start. Whom then did their untimely deaths benefit? All true nationalists should pause and think! (p. 194)

Ngugi is on the side of the people – of African 'populism' and against capitalism. For Ngugi:

> Capitalism and imperialism are the root causes of evil. Our economy is dependent on international capitalism. And capitalism can never bring about equality of peoples. The exploitation of one group by another is the very essence of capitalism. The peasants and workers are very much exploited in this country. They get very low pay, very poor housing, and unemployment affects them more than anyone else. Now, women form the majority in this category of peasants. Women are doubly exploited and oppressed. It's general third-world problem.
>
> Workers and peasants and women form the most important element in this country. They are the true producers of wealth. They produce all the wealth that feeds, clothes, houses everyone in the society. They also produce all the wealth that goes out of the country. Yet they do not get even the barest minimum of that which they produced. The middle class that feeds on the workers and peasants is a superfluous, parasitic class.

Ngugi's position, then, is closest to Karega and is bound up with questions of education. Education is discussed a good deal in the novel and four of the principal characters, Munira, Karega, Chui and Mzigo, are teachers. Once again the complexities and coincidences of the relationships between characters play a vital thematic part in the narrative structure. Chui and Munira have been schoolboys together at Siriana. Chui is something of a legend as a scholar and a sportsman. And it is he who leads a strike against the pedagogy of the headmaster, Fraudsham. Chui causes so much bother that he is sent overseas to complete his education there. And the pattern of Chui's life repeats itself in Karega. Karega in the succeeding generation leads a strike to have Fraudsham fired. This time the strike succeeds and Fraudsham is deposed, replaced as the irony of fate has it by Chui. Karega and his classmates anticipate a new beginning, a reform of the curriculum, ultimately a 'new People'. But Chui arrives, 'a black replica of Fraudsham', re-affirming what for Karega and his fellows are the outworn traditions of cultivating an alien culture at the school.

For Chui this is but the first step on the road to becoming an investor in the foreign exploitation of his country. For Karega it is the beginning of his quest for a purpose in his life connected to ameliorating the lives of the exploited masses. It must be done, he conceives, through education. But he wrestles with what kind of education it should be. His sense of purpose is confirmed when in a hallucinatory, Theng'eta – induced dream, he encounters his long dead brother, Nding'uri. The quest of the Mau Mau, identical with the quest of the contempory peasants and workers, is to get the land back. Karega shouts after Nding'uri: 'I want to follow you!'

Nding'uri stops and he is now both weary and angry.

> 'What kind of teacher are you? Leave your children adrift? The struggle, brother, starts where you are.' (p. 237)

But the question of how to advance the struggle exercises Karega. He seeks through formal learning to find truths which he can convey to his pupils. He turns to history, political science and literature for answers – but he finds none there. The reasons why this is so are not hard to find – though it is the lawyer, the shadowy and ambiguous figure the marchers have met in Nairobi – who points out certain fallacies and fallibilities in formal learning to Karega:

> 'You had asked me for books written by Black Professors. I wanted you to judge for yourself. Educators, men of letters, intellectuals: these are only voices – not neutral, disembodied voices – but belonging to bodies of persons, of groups, of interest. You, who will seek the truth about words emitted by a voice, look first for the body behind the voice. The voice merely rationalises the needs, whims, caprices, of its owner, the master. Better therefore to know the master in whose service the intellect is and you'll be able to properly evaluate the import and imagery of his utterances. You serve the people who struggle; or you serve those who rob the people. In a situation of the robber and the robbed, in a situation in which the old man of the sea is sitting on Sindbad, there can be no neutral history and politics. If you would learn look about you: choose your side.' (p. 200)

Karega's bewilderment over the failure of formal learning to provide the sort of answers he needs seem an anagram of Ngugi's own disillusion-ment. The names he associates with the formal inquiries of history, political science and literature are scholars from his own country. And provided he summarizes accurately the nature of their implied statements on the uses of history, political science and literature, we see a dimension of Ngugi's assertion that at the root of the failure of these disciplines to serve the needs of the people is the fact that they are undertaken – indeed must be undertaken – in a foreign language.

But whatever his disillusions, Karega's procedures as a teacher are shown to contrast in a favourable light with Munira's throughout the period of their association. Whereas Munira believes that pupils should be given 'simple facts. Information, just so they can pass their CPE', Karega disputes this claim:

'I cannot accept that there is a stage in our growth as human beings when all we need are so-called facts and information. Man is a thinking being from the time he is born to the time he dies. He looks, he hears, he touches, he smells, he tastes and he sifts all these impressions in his mind to arrive at a certain outlook in his direct experience of life. Are there pure facts? When I am looking at you, how much I see of you is conditioned by where I stand or sit; by the amount of light in this room; by the power of my eyes; by whether my mind is occupied with other thoughts and what thoughts. Surely the story we teach about the seven blind men who had never seen an elephant is instructive. Looking and touching, then, do involve interpretation. Even assuming that there were pure facts, what about their selection? Does this not involve interpretation?' (p. 246)

For Karega learning and teaching are inseparable: 'In teaching the children, he had sensed a possible vocation, a daily dialogue with his deepest self, as he tried to understand the children and the world which shaped their future and their chances in life' (p. 252). And even though he abandons formal learning and formal teaching, saying perhaps too naively – 'besides, what else was there to learn besides what he had experienced with his eyes and hands?' (p. 302) – his mission as a union leader will be as a teacher since he will have to convey the truth to the peasants and workers that there has to be a choice between capitalism and socialism and, more important and more difficult for him, what and why that choice must be.

Ngugi's rendering of history is consistent with his political purposes in the novel and follows a process of evolution as Marx describes it – from feudal to bourgeois – capitalist and proletarian. In *Petals of Blood* his analysis is at the stage where class antagonism between the capitalist and proletariat is polarized. Unlike Marx, Ngugi celebrates Africa's glorious past in numerous passages in the novel. But he is also pragmatic in recognizing that history, the contemplation of the past, offers no short cuts to the solution to problems in the present. Solutions which make for the brighter future will come at the end of a long and arduous class struggle.

The class struggle will have its origins in the peasantry and in the third part of the novel Ngugi draws more on traditional verbal material than elsewhere in his writing. Ngugi uses it to enforce a sense of communality derived from custom and a system of village ethics which suppresses individualism in the interest of the common good. We see at the ceremony of making the first Theng'eta, wherein Njuguna and Nyakinyua provide an 'opera of eros', perhaps the last manifestation of a group of villagers acting in a communal way. The young and the old, celebrating the harvest, form a circle and move to the rhythm of the chanting of Njuguna and Nyakinyua and act as a chorus to the ceremony they perform in mime and song. The history of the village and the villagers moves forward from the dim mists of early time through to the present and the changes which rend the society apart form the last segment of her song:

> They listened to Nyakinyua as she sang Gitiro. At first it was good-humoured, light-hearted, as she commented on those present to a chorus of laughter.
> But suddenly they were caught by the slight tremor in her voice. She was singing their recent history. She sang of two years of failing rains; of the arrival of daughters and teachers; of the exodus to the city. She talked of how she had earlier imagined the city as containing only wealth. But she found poverty; she found crippled beggars; she saw men, many men, sons of women, vomited out of a smoking tunnel – a big, big house – and she was afraid. Who had swallowed all the wealth of the land? Who?
> And now it was no longer the drought of a year ago that she was singing about. It was all the droughts of the centuries and the journey was the many journeys travelled by people even in the mythical lands of two-mouthed Marimus and struggling humans. She sang of other struggles, of other wars – the arrival of colonialism and the fierce struggles waged against it by newly circumcised youth. Yes, it was always the duty of youth to drive out foreigners and enemies lodged amongst the people: it was always the duty of youth to fight all the Marimus, all the two-mouthed Ogres, and that was the meaning of the blood shed at circumcision. (pp. 209–10)

And in the recapitulation of the history of his people Karega recognizes the force of traditional ethics and the beauty of the history of the people Nyakinyua sings about. But in the end the account has no relevance in the present. Says Karega:

> It was really very beautiful. But at the end of the evening Karega felt very sad. It was like beholding a relic of beauty that had suddenly surfaced, or like listening to a solitary beautiful tune straying, for a time, from a dying world. (p. 210)

For Karega the struggle is in the future and he is moved to recognize the past is of no use to the present struggle:

Even in himself he could not recognize the dreamer who once could talk endlessly about Africa's past glories, Africa's great feudal cultures, as if it was enough to have this knowledge to cure one day's pang of hunger, to quench an hour's thirst or to clothe a naked child. After all, the British merchant magnates and their missionary soothsayers once colonised and humiliated China by making the Chinese buy and drink opium and clubbed them when they refused to import the poison, even while the British scholars sang of China's great feudal cultures and stole the evidence in gold and art and parchments and took them to London. Egypt too. India too. Syria, Iraq ... God was born in Palestine even ... and all this knowledge never once deterred the European merchant warlords. And China was saved, not by singers and poets telling of great past cultures, but by the creative struggle of the workers for a better day today. No, it was not a people's past glories only, but also the glory of their present strife and struggles to right the wrongs that bring tears to the many and laughter only to a few. The Ilmorog whose past achievements had moved him so after listening to Nyakinyua was not there any more. (pp. 301–2)

The book is open to the charge of political attitudinizing in places, but generally the political attitudes Ngugi strikes and political questions he examines through the events in the novel and the actions of the characters are balanced by his humanism. This attitude or quality can be summed up best in Karega's statement to Wanja:

'Whenever any of us is degraded and humiliated, even the smallest child, we are all humiliated and degraded because it has got to do with human beings.' (p. 161)

At the end of the novel there is hope – for Wanja and for her child by Abdulla; for Abdulla who has at last found a kind of peace for himself in recognizing that:

history was a dance in a huge arena of God. You played your part, whatever your chosen part, and then you left the arena, swept aside by the waves of a new step, a new movement in the dance. Other dancers, younger, brighter, more inventive came and played with even greater skill, with more complicated footwork, before they too were swept aside by yet a greater tide in the movement they had helped to create, and other dancers were thrown up to carry the dance to even newer heights and possibilities undreamt of by an earlier generation. (p. 340)

And the metaphor is worked out in the life of Joseph who, ironically, repeats the cycle in which Munira and Chui, and Karega were involved. Joseph is at Siriana. His catalogue of complaints about Chui's regime are reminiscent of those of Chui and later Karega. And his aspirations are like those of Karega. He says to Abdulla:

'When I grow up and finish school and university I want to be like you: I would like to feel proud that I had done something for our people. You fought for the political independence of this country: I would like to contribute to the liberation of the people of this country. I have been reading a lot about Mau Mau: I hope that one day we shall make Karuna-ini, where Kimathi was born, and Othaya, where J.M. was born, national shrines. And build a theatre in memory of Kimathi, because as a teacher he organised the Gichamu Theatre Movement in Tetu . . . I have been reading a lot about what the workers and peasants of other lands have done in history. I have read about the people's revolutions in China, Cuba, Vietnam, Cambodia, Laos, Angola, Guinea, Mozambique . . . Oh yes, and the works of Lenin and Mao . . . '(pp. 339–40)

If Joseph stays the pace the pronouncement of Nding'uri in the dream will be fulfilled.

Finally there is hope in the solidarity among workers and peasants which emerges in the New Ilmorog. In this Karega sees the possibility of reversing the patterns of history which has brought the 'Blackman' to his knees. Karega sees in the beginnings of this nationalist movement a pattern epitomized in his drugged dream:

Today, children, I am going to tell you about the history of Mr Blackman in three sentences. In the beginning he had the land and the mind and the soul together. On the second day, they took the body away to barter it for silver coins. On the third day, seeing that he was still fighting back, they brought priests and educators to bind his mind and soul so that these foreigners could more easily take his land and its produce. And now I shall ask you a question: what has Mr Blackman done to attain the true kingdom of his earth? To bring back his mind and soul and body together on his piece of earth? They are actually – how strange – on a raft of banana stems drifting across oceans of time and space. And he is no longer Mwalimu but Chaka leading induna after induna against the Foreign invader. He is L'Ouverture, discarding the comfort and the wealth and the false security of a house slave to throw his intellect and muscles at the feet of the field slaves ready for a united people's struggle against the drinkers of human sweat, eaters of human flesh. Children, he calls out: see this new African without chains on his legs, without chains on his mind, without chains in his soul, a proud warrior-producer in three continents. And they see him over and over in new guises Koitalel, Waiyaki, Nat Turner, Cinque, Kimathi, Cabral, Nkrumah, Nasser, Mondhlane, Mathenge – radiating the same message, the same possibilities, the same cry and hope of a million Africans . . . (pp. 236–7)

But the hope Karega feels is circumscribed by the existence of Nderi wa Riera, the MP for Ilmorog, and also the organizer and controller of an association known as the KCO, 'the most feared instrument of selective but coercive terror in the land' (p. 186), an organization supported by the police and which owes its existence to the police. Godfrey is the servant of the established political regime. This is the regime of repressive and corrupt people like Nderi wa Riera.

Nderi wa Riera began well in public life but he quickly succumbed to the blandishments of directors of the various organizations of International Finance Capitalism. His path, as Ngugi describes it, is one which many have followed:

> He would champion such populist causes as putting a ceiling on land ownership; nationalisation of the major industries and commercial enterprises; abolition of illiteracy and unemployment and the East African Federation as a step to Pan-African Unity.
> Then he was flooded with offers of directorships in foreign-owned companies. 'Mr Riera, you need not do anything: we do not want to take too much of your busy and valuable time. It is only that we believe in white and black partnership for real progress.' The money he had collected from his constituents for a water project was not enough for piped water. But it was adequate as a security for further loans until he bought shares in companies and invested in land, in housing and in small business. He suddenly dropped out of circulation in small places. Now he could only be found in special clubs for members only, or in newspapers – photographed while attending this or that cocktail party. As if to reinforce his new social standing, he took a huge farm in the Rift Valley. But his most lucrative connection was with the tourist industry. He owned a number of plots and premises in Mombasa, Malindi and Watamu and had been given shares in several tourist resorts all along the coast. Soon he began talking of 'the need for people to grow up and face reality. Africa needed capital investment for real growth – not socialist slogans'. (p. 174)

The KCO is founded for the purpose of protecting these interests.

Inspector Godfrey knows Nderi as corrupt and is moved to list in his mind the extent and ugliness of that corruption. Ultimately, however, Godfrey is 'a crime detective not the leader of a moral vice squad . . . How silly of him to have let himself be drawn into moral questions of how and why'.

More than this he:

> had been brought up to believe in the sanctity of private property. The system of private ownership, of means of production, exchange and distribution, was for him synonymous with the natural order of things like the sun, the moon and the stars which seemed fixed and permanent in the firmament. Anybody who interfered with that ordained fixity and permanence of things was himself unnatural and deserved no mercy: was he not inviting chaos such as would occur if some foolish astronaut/cosmonaut should go and push the sun or the moon from its place? (p. 333)

Thus for Godfrey:

> People like Karega with their radical trade unionism and communism threatened the very structure of capitalism: as such they were worse than murderers. (p. 333)

The struggle will need to continue in the face of opposition as

formidable as that represented by Nderi and Godfrey. Karega's assertion
to Wanja's is true:

'They are bound to fail. Can't you see: we, the workers, the poor peasants,
ordinary people, the masses are now too awake to be deceived about tribal
loyalties, regional assemblies, glorious pasts, utamaduni wa zamani, all that –
when we are starving and we are jobless, or else living on miserable pay. Do you
think we shall let foreign companies, banks, insurances – all that – and the local
rich with their Theng'eta companies, the new black landlords with their
massive land-holdings and numerous houses – do you think people will let a
combination of these two classes and their spokesmen in parliament, at
universities, in schools, in churches and with all their armies and police to
guard their interests – do you think that we shall let these owners of stolen
property continue lording it over us for ever? No. . . it is too late, Wanja . . . we
shall no longer let others reap where they never planted, harvest where they
never cultivated, take to their banks from where they never sweated . . . Tell
them this: There are a million Karegas for every ten Kimerias. They can kill the
lawyer or ten such lawyers. But the poor, the dispossessed, the working millions
and the poor peasants are their own lawyers. With guns and swords and
organisation, they can and will change the conditions of their oppression.
They'll seize the wealth which rightly belongs to them. Why – it's happening all
around us – Mozambique, Angola, Zimbabwe. Just now you thought I was not
touched by your grandfather's story. I would choose your grandfather ten
times . . . not your father . . . Never! The workers and the peasant farmers of
Kenya are awake.' (pp. 326–7)

The language is that of the Marxist revolutionary who accepts the odds
and who recognizes that the struggle will be long and hard. It is a
statement reinforced throughout the novel in such stark references as to
'all the black toiling masses carrying a jembe in one hand and three bullets
in the other, struggling against centuries of drifting, sole witness of their
own homecoming'. Ngugi's debt to Marx is transmuted into fiction in his
descriptions of the circumstances by which alienation of the peasant
from his land takes place and of the social economic conditions which
arise out of this, conditions which prompt the revolution. Ngugi has
debts to other mentors that support the artistic presentation he offers us
in the novel. In common with Zola, Ngugi expresses concern for a mass of
people consigned to poverty and exploitation, a humanist seeking
political solutions to awful political problems. In common with Conrad is
Ngugi's willingness to face squarely mankind's imperfections, his sus-
ceptibility to corruption, his proneness to violence. Implicit in his
evocation of contemporary Kenya is a recognition of the need for order
and restraint and for harmony in the total population. We see too Ngugi's
debt to poets of Apocalyptic vision – Whitman and Blake and Yeats. For
Ngugi as for Blake the church is the whore of the state and does nothing to

alleviate circumstances that produce the youthful harlot's curse which blasts the new born Infant's tear. And the Bethlehem toward which the peasants from Ilmorog slouch in the second part of the novel is a Bethlehem – call it Nairobi or New Ilmorog – derived from the anguished prophetic vision of Yeats, the disillusion of civilization, the home not of Christ in a Second Coming but of anti-Christ. Yeats' words have an exact appropriateness to the spirit and the circumstances which are unleashed in the land and epitomized in the creation of the New Ilmorog.

It is against this creation, vision and spirit, epitomized by Yeats' vision of the anti-Christ of the 'second-coming' that Karega and his cohorts must contend.

Set against Ngugi's depiction of the desecration of the landscape are passages of lyrical exuberance in their evocation of the land. Attitudes to the land, to its uses, proprietorship, but to its very substance are conveyed for many points of view throughout the book. Land is life. And while there is not the consistent use of motifs in the novel (in any of his novels), relating natural elements to the fundamental human problems one might expect to find as one finds elsewhere in modern African writing, these elements exist. Ngugi uses natural elements to help to define human relations. So of the unsatisfactory liaison of Wanja and Munira on the night Wanja hopes to become pregnant at the time of the full moon, Ngugi writes:

> If Wanja had been patient and had waited for the new moon to appear on New Ilmorog ridge – as indeed she had been instructed by Mwathi wa Mugo – she and Munira would have witnessed one of the most glorious and joyous sights in all the land, with the ridges and the plains draped by a level sheet of shimmering moonlit mist into a harmony of peace and silence: a human soul would have to be restless and raging beyond reach of hope and salvation for it not to be momentarily overwhelmed and stilled by the sight and the atmosphere. (p. 67)

But a harmonious conjunction between nature and humanity is found in the union between Wanja and Karega. Their happiness is revealed to Munira to whom a similar happiness was denied:

> Of an evening I saw them together across the fields, stumbling over mikengeria creepers, over yellow merry-golden flowers, over the tall thangari stem grass, bringing back thistles on the back and front and the sides of their clothes. Often, they would walk across Ilmorog ridge, two distant shadows against the golden glow of the setting sun, and disappear behind the hill to come back in the darkness or in the moonlight.
>
> Their love seemed to grow with the new crops of the year.
>
> They were still a-wandering across Ilmorog country, always together in the fields, on the mountain-top, in the plains, their love blossoming in the wind, as if both were re-enacting broken possibilities in their pasts. (pp. 244–5)

Passages similar in kind can be found throughout the novel, as here on the march to the city where physical forces conspire, as it were, to compromise belief in the superior strength and independence of human-kind and where that strength is hallowed by connection with generations past:

> They did not know it, but that night was to be the peak of their epic journey across the plains. It was true that Abdulla's feast, as they called it, had leased them new life and determination, and the following day, despite the sun which had struck earlier and more fiercely than in the other days, as if to test their capacity for endurance to the very end, despite indeed the evidence of the acacia bush, the ashy-furred leleshwa bush, the prickly pears, all of which seemed to have given in to the bitter sun, they walked with brisk steps as if they too knew this secret desire of the sun and were resolved to come out on top. Abdulla's story had made them aware of a new relationship to the ground on which they trod: the ground, the murram grass, the agapanthas, the cactus, everything in the plains, had been hallowed by the feet of those who had fought and died that Kenya might be free: wasn't there something, a spirit of those people in them too?

The conjunction between nature and human life as suggested most amply in the implications of the title of the book itself. *Petals of Blood* is a phrase found in a poem by Derek Walcott, the West Indian poet and playwright, called 'The Swamp'. The lines read:

> Fearful, original sinuosities! Each mangrove sapling
> Serpentlike, its roots obscene
> As a six-fingered hand,
>
> Conceals within its clutch the mossbacked toad,
> Toadstools, the potent ginger-lily,
> Petals of blood,
>
> The speckled vulva of the tiger-orchid:
> Outlandish phalloi
> Haunting the travellers of its one road.[4]

Ngugi says that in the 'very huge tree [that] prevents little flowers from reaching out into the light'[5] is suggested a metaphor of the way 'in which the social system of capitalism and imperialism act to stifle life'[6]. But there is more to it than this. The verses suggest the existence of forces – symbolized by the physical objects of toads and toadstools and tiger-orchids – associated with death and danger which makes man's pilgrimage perilous. There is also the suggestion of aberrant birth arising out of unrestrained sexuality. In this connection the imagery of the Walcott poem suggests that employed by Yeats in his 'The Second Coming'. Walcott's lines imply that there is a deadly force in nature which threatens mankind, and the implications of the poem – in the network of association Ngugi derives from the phrase – stand juxtaposed with those forces in nature which are in harmony with man. Mankind can look to the sweeping vision of sun-drenched plains and valleys for a vision of his connection with the heavens. But he must, as well, be constantly on guard for the lurking danger at his feet. In the novel the phrase, 'Petals of Blood', applies not only to the harmless bean flower the children discover in their natural science lesson at the beginning of the novel, but also to the 'very small plant with a pattern of four tiny red petals' from which 'Theng'eta – The Spirit' is made. And Theng'eta called variously 'Drink of Peace', 'Drink of Strife', and 'Deadly Lotus' – becomes the agent of hallucinatory revelations which prompt division between the four principal characters creating strife where at least a semblance of peace prevailed. Ultimately it is mass-produced, distributed in various consistencies overseas for capital gain by Mzigo. And it is supplied to the workers to deaden their pain, dull their recognition – an opiate as deadly and useless to their need as the Christian church or the charismatic movement. Thus the association of 'Petals of Blood' and the 'Song' by Josh White, which the lawyer hums in the recounting to Karega his travels in America, is made plain, and the connection with 'Third World', the black diaspora mentioned throughout the novel is enhanced:

Southern trees
Bear strange fruits
Blood around the leaves
And blood at the roots
Black body swaying
In a Southern breeze
Strange fruit
Hanging from poplar trees. (p. 165)

Ngugi's characters seek ways to give meaning to their lives in a world where customary values and props have been abandoned, repudiated, even made mock of. The younger generation, Karega and Joseph, pin their faith on political solutions as a means of combating the hatred, intolerance, tribalism and corruption which flourish. Moreover, Ngugi suggests in the hope we have for Wanja and the child she will bear that love, friendship and decent human relations may flourish. Just as surely he suggests that the response made by Munira is hopeless. It is appropriate, too, that Nyakinyua dies when she does – she has lived out her span and what she stands for and what she lived by are no longer valued or appropriate. When the homestead of the traditional sage, Mugo wa Mwathi, was driven at by bulldozers all of the villagers expected death and destruction to follow. But the building gave way to the blades. The sage had fled. Nyakinyua's time had passed.

Petals of Blood affirms the consistency of Ngugi's themes and attitudes. To what was outlined in the first two novels and elaborated further in the third have been added the harsh attitude of the prose writing of recent years as Ngugi has contemplated what for him was a deteriorating scene of treachery and betrayal around him. The novel closes by posing the implicit questions: 'can people do anything to reverse their positions as helpless victims, will they take the means that are to hand?'

REFERENCES AND NOTES

1. 'Ngugi interviewed by Magina Magina', in *Africa Report*, No. 90 (February 1979), pp. 30-1.
2. 'Ngugi interviewed by Anita Shrev', in *Viva* (July 1977), p. 35.
3. *Ibid.*
4. Derek Walcott, 'The Swamp' in *The Castaway and Other Poems* London, Jonathan Cape, 1965).
5. *Ibid*, p. 36.
6. *Ibid*, p. 35.

Bibliography

The Works of Ngugi wa Thiong'o

NOVELS

The River Between (London: Heinemann, 1965, reset 1975). All page references in the text refer to the reset edition.

Weep Not, Child (London: Heinemann, 1964, reset 1976). All page references in the text refer to the reset edition.

A Grain of Wheat (London: Heinemann, 1967, reset 1975). All page references in the text refer to the reset edition.

Petals of Blood (London: Heinemann, 1977).

PLAYS

The Black Hermit (London: Heinemann, 1968, reprinted 1979).

The Trial of Dedan Kimathi (London: Heinemann, 1976). (Written with Micere Mugo).

'This Time Tomorrow' in Cosmo Pieterse (ed.) *Short African Plays* (London: Heinemann, 1972, reprinted 1978).

SHORT STORIES

Secret Lives (London: Heinemann, 1975, reprinted 1979).

ESSAYS

Homecoming (London: Heinemann, 1972).

Secondary Sources

INTERVIEWS

Abdullahai, Aminu, in *African Writers Talking* (London: Heinemann, 1972).

Pieterse, Cosmo and Duerden, Dennis, in *African Writers Talking* (London: Heinemann, 1972).

Sander, Reinhard and Munro, Ian, 'Tolstoy in Africa', *Ba Shiru*, Vol. 5 (1973).

ARTICLES

Cook, David, 'A new earth: a study of James Ngugi's *A Grain of Wheat*', *East Africa Journal*, Vol. 6, No. 12 (1969).

Ikiddeh, Ime, 'James Ngugi as novelist', *African Literature Today*, Nos. 1-4 (collected) (London: Heinemann, 1969).

Martini, Jürgen, 'Ngugi wa Thiong'o: East African novelist', paper given at the ACLALS meeting (European branch) in Rabat (Malta) (March 1978).

Obumselu, Ebele (Ben), 'Marx, politics and the African novel', *Twentieth Century Studies*, Vol. 10 (1973).

Obumselu, Ben, '*A Grain of Wheat*: Ngugi's debt to Conrad', *Benin Review*, Vol. 1 (1974).

Okenimpke, Michael, 'Culture and revolution in the novels of James Ngugi', Association for Commonwealth Literature and Language Studies, *Bulletin No. 10* (June 1972).

Rauch, Ericka, 'The central male-female relationship in *The River Between* and *Mission to Kala*', *Busara*, Vol. 7, No. 1 (1975).

Ravenscroft, Arthur, 'Ngugi's development as a novelist', *Commonwealth* (Aarhus, 1972).

Rice, Michael, '*The River Between* – a discussion', *English in Africa*, Vol. 2 (1975).

Sander, Reinhard, 'Two views of the conflict of culture in pre-emergency Kenya', *The Literary Half-Year*, Vol. XIX, No. 2 (Delhi, 1978).

Williams, Lloyd, 'Religion and life in James Ngugi's *The River Between*', *African Literature Today*, Vol. 5 (London: Heinemann, 1971).

CHAPTERS IN BOOKS

Gakwandi, Shatto Arthur, 'Ngugi's *A Grain of Wheat* and Sembene Ousmane's *God's Bits of Wood*' in *The Novel and Contemporary Experience in Africa* (London: Heinemann, 1977).

Ikiddeh, Ime, 'Ngugi wa Thiong'o: the novelist as historian' in Bruce King and Kolawole Ogungbesan (eds.), *A Celebration of Black African Writing* (Zaria: Ahmodu Bello University Press; London: OUP, 1975).

Monkman, Leslie, 'Kenya and the New Jerusalem in *A Grain of Wheat*', *African Literature Today*, No. 7 (London: Heinemann, 1975).

Nazareth, Peter, '*A Grain of Wheat*: a socialist novel?' in *Literature and Society in Modern Africa* (Nairobi: East African Literature Bureau, 1972).

Index

▼▼▼▼▼▼▼▼▼▼▼▼▼▼▼▼▼▼▼▼▼▼▼▼▼▼▼▼▼▼▼▼

DATE DUE